# Drama Scripts

~~~~~

# Radio

## Liz Wainwright

*Somebody*

*A Second Summer*

*Madame*

*Mrs Danby's Destiny*

Createspace for
Loveday Manor Publishing
www.lizscript.co.uk

ISBN-10: 1477604162
ISBN-13: 978-1477604168

# DEDICATION

For Glyn
and
Our wonderful family

# CONTENTS

# ACKNOWLEDGMENTS

Thank you to Glyn for the book design.
The interior layout, typesetting, and page format  is based on original
studio script texts and radio drama layouts.

# SOMEBODY

By

## Liz Wainwright

Original Production
Directed by Marion Nancarrow
BBC Radio 4 Drama
Broadcast 1998
Running Time: 55m

Cast:

| | |
|---|---|
| Eileen | Lynda Bellingham |
| Roy | David Ross |
| Jenny | Kate Fenwick |
| Nick/Christophe | Charles Simpson |
| Samantha | Sarah-Jane Holm |
| Janice | Frances Jeater |

## **SCENE 1 - (PROLOGUE).**

1. EILEEN:   V/O: It's pathetic isn't it when you're grateful for an elasticated waist.

(LAUGHS) What with Roy's beer belly and my rear-end we must have looked like a couple of blueberry muffins in those baggy jeans we bought.

2. ROY:   V/O: Me and Eileen went on holiday to America to celebrate our Silver Wedding. Everything was wonderful, till I read that sign about the Cherokee.

I couldn't get it out of my mind.

(PAUSE) Do you know, the last time I can remember being happy was on that holiday.

## SCENE 2 (F/B 1).

F/X: A QUIET STREET IN SMALL TOWN
AMERICA. CRICKETS, OCCASIONAL
TRUCK PASSES. A CAR PULLS UP, AND
MUSIC IS HEARD THROUGH ITS OPEN
WINDOWS FROM THE CAR'S CASSETTE
PLAYER. MUSIC: JACKSON (JOHNNY
CASH AND JUNE CARTER.)

1. ROY:     Do you think we can park here?

2. EILEEN;  I don't see why not.

         F/X: RADIO TURNED OFF. CAR DOORS
         OPENED AND CLOSED.

3. EILEEN:  Oh, I could do with a drink. There's a café over there, Roy.

4. ROY:     Ma Barker's - sounds good to me, honey!

5. EILEEN:  Bryson City. I don't know how they can call one street a city.

6. ROY:     No, there's not a lot here, is there?

7. EILEEN:  Shall we have a quick meal and then try somewhere else? There's a place called Nantahala a bit further on.

8. ROY:     Nantahala! Cherokee country! No, let's stick with Bill Bryson, I want to stay in that motel. Hey, there it is, just like in the book.

1. EILEEN:    (DOUBTFUL) Oh, is that it?   What about the
             motel opposite, that looks pretty.  Let's have a
             look at that one before we decide.  But I must
             have a drink first.

             <u>FX: FADE UP DRUM BEAT - INDIAN</u>

             <u>DRUMS (FIVE BEATS, ONE, 2 & 3,4?)</u>

2. EILEEN:    (DISTANT)  Roy, come on.

3. ROY:       Just a minute, love.  I'm reading this. 'Tsali.
             Cherokee brave surrendered to General Scott to
             be shot near here, 1838, that remnant of his
             tribe might remain in North Carolina'.

             <u>F/X:   FADE UP DRUM BEAT</u>

             <u>TITLES</u>

## SCENE 3.

EILEEN'S LIVING ROOM IN A SMALL
TERRACED COTTAGE.

F/X: EILEEN IS HOOVERING.

CASSETTE PLAYING, 'SURFIN' USA' (THE
BEACH BOYS)

JENNY KNOCKS AT THE COTTAGE DOOR
AND WALKS STRAIGHT IN.

1. JENNY:   Mum! Mum!

          F/X: HOOVER SWITCHED OFF

2. EILEEN:   Oh, hello, love. I didn't expect to see you today.

3. JENNY:   Nick sent me out for a break, Daniel woke up too early and hasn't stopped grizzling all morning.

4. EILEEN:   Oh, let's hope he's better tomorrow. Have a sit down and I'll make you a cup of tea. You don't want this on, do you?

F/X: TURNS TAPE OFF

5. JENNY:   Is that one of the tapes you bought in America?

6. EILEEN:   No, it's an old one of your Dad's.

          I suppose I should give it him back really. I'll put the kettle on.

<u>EILEEN GOES TO THE ADJACENT
KITCHEN AND CARRIES ON THE
CONVERSATION FROM THERE.</u>

<u>F/X: KETTLE FILLED, CUPS ETC</u>

1. EILEEN: Have you heard from Nick's parents?

2. JENNY: Oh, yes. They couldn't cancel their 'prior arrangement' after all.

3. EILEEN: Oh. Is Nick upset?

4. JENNY: Yes. You can't call them grandparents, can you, if they can't be bothered to come to their grandson's first birthday?

5. EILEEN: Not everyone wants to be a Grandma and Grandad.

<u>(EILEEN COMES IN WITH CUPS ETC)</u>

Your Dad wasn't keen at first, if you remember. Do you want a biscuit?

6. JENNY: Thanks. Dad's made up for it since, though. And he's delighted I'm expecting again.

7. EILEEN: Yes, he would be. He always wished we'd not just had the one.

8. JENNY: Nick's really pleased that Dad's started coming round more since you and he . . .

9. EILEEN: Well, I'm glad somebody's benefited - besides me, of course.

10. JENNY: Nick and I were saying, it'd be nice if our kids could have at least one proper set of grandparents.

1.EILEEN: What do you mean?

2.JENNY: (LIGHT) Well, we'd like them to have a Nan and Grandad, together. You know, like I'd like a Mum and Dad instead of Roy and Eileen living apart.

3. EILEEN: Don't start, Jennifer.

4. JENNY: Sorry. How are things at work? Have they finished the grand re-structuring yet?

### F/X: SHE GETS THE TEA

5. EILEEN: Yes, till the next time. I wish they'd try a bit of common sense instead of paying all these consultants.

6. JENNY: You'll be able to think about having a break then, now it's all sorted out.

7. EILEEN: In theory, yes. Michelle brought some travel brochures into work yesterday for me and the girls to look at.

8. JENNY: Oh, are you going away with them?

9. EILEEN: No, I don't think so.

10. JENNY: A winter break would be nice, though, wouldn't it?

11. EILEEN: Oh, yes, I'd love to get away, but I'll have to wait till I've saved up a bit.

12.JENNY: Dad was talking about a holiday.

13.EILEEN: Oh?

14.JENNY: No fun going on your own though, is it?

15.EILEEN: No, I suppose not.

1.JENNY: I'd better get back and rescue Nick - he can only manage the New Man ethic in short bursts. Oh, he wants to know if you'll be giving Dad a lift.

2. EILEEN: Of course I will.

3. JENNY: See you tomorrow then. Wear your party frock!

> F/X:  JENNY EXITS.  PAUSE.  EILEEN TAKES THE TAPE  OUT OF THE BOX AND PLAYS IT AGAIN.  END OF 'SURFIN USA',
>
> NEXT TRACK BEGINS -'SLOOP JOHN B'

4. EILEEN: V/O:  They have these Golden Oldies radio stations in America.  That was what me and Roy used to listen to, or Country and Western.

That holiday was a present from our Jenny and Nick, and my sister, Janice for our 25th anniversary.  That's well over a year ago now.

It was a fantastic experience, we couldn't get over the space, and the enthusiasm.

(PAUSE) That was one of the things I used to love about Roy, his enthusiasm.

We went to Nashville and we drove along the Parkway through the Blue Ridge Mountains.

Then for the rest of the holiday we stayed with Janice and her husband. They live near Washington.

(PAUSE)  Something happened to Roy that holiday - I don't know what.

> F/X:  FADE UP DRUM BEAT

## SCENE 4.

NICK AND JENNY'S LOUNGE. F/X: FADE
OUT THE DRUM AND FADE UP ROY
QUIETLY PLAYING A TOY DRUM.

1. ROY:      Not bad quality is it, for a toy?

2. NICK:     No, and Daniel loves it.

3. ROY:      I bet you won't love it if he starts playing it at
             five o'clock in the morning. You won't love me,
             either, for buying it!

4. NICK:     No, probably not.

5. ROY:      (STOPS PLAYING) I'll tell her as soon as they
             come back down.

6. NICK:     How do you think she'll react.

7. ROY:      She'll be over the moon. A free holiday. You
             can't turn that down. Can you?

8. NICK:     You should have told her about it before,
             though.

9. ROY:      Like I said, I'd forgotten all about it, till I got the
             letter. Anyway, with Eileen it's better to just do
             what you want and let her argue with you
             afterwards. Me and Jennifer worked that out a
             long time ago.

10. NICK:    Can I get you another beer?

11. ROY:     No, I'll wait for the champagne. Do you think I
             should announce it with a drum roll as well?

             F/X: ROY BEGINS TO PLAY THE TOY
             DRUM AGAIN AS EILEEN AND JENNY

## ENTER WHISPERING AND CLOSING THE
## LOUNGE DOOR VERY CAREFULLY.

1. JENNY: (QUIETLY) Typical! Up half the night and then he can't stay awake to blow out his candle. Dad, shush, you'll wake him up.

2. ROY: Oh, sorry.

3. EILEEN: I can't believe you bought him a drum, Roy. We agreed Lego.

4. ROY: And we got Lego. But I knew he'd like a drum as well.

5. EILEEN: You didn't think about Nicholas and our Jennifer having to listen to it, though.

6. JENNY: It's OK Mum.

7. ROY: Pity he didn't blow his candle out, I was looking forward to making a wish.

8. EILEEN: It's only the birthday boy who can make a wish.

9. ROY: I don't see why. It's nice for everybody to join in. I bet I know what you'd wish for, Eileen.

10. EILEEN: What?

11. ROY: The same as me.

12. EILEEN: (PAUSE) And what's that?

13. ROY: A damned good holiday.

14. EILEEN: (DISAPPOINTED) Oh. Shall I put the cake back in the tin, Jenny?

15. JENNY: No, we can have some now - as long as we leave the part with the candle in it. I think we should open the champagne now, Nick.

1. NICK:     Yes, get your glasses ready.

2. EILEEN:   Oh, yes we can still have the birthday toast.

3. JENNY:    You've something else to celebrate, as well.

4. EILEEN:   What?

5.ROY:       Me and Jenny have got a surprise for you.  Do you remember me getting that free copy of an over 50s magazine?

6.EILEEN:    I remember you moaning about it.

7.ROY:       'Que Sera' it was called.  Well, I entered the holiday competition that was in it.

8.EILEEN:    You didn't tell me.

9.ROY:       Well, it was just before we . . .

10. JENNY:   Anyway you've won one of the prizes!  It's either a cruise - that's the first prize, of course, or a fortnight on a Greek island or a week in the South of France.

            F/X:  CHAMPAGNE CORK POPS.  NICK

            FILLS THEIR GLASSES.

12. ROY:     You and me haven't had a proper holiday since America, have we, Eileen?  Won't it be great!

13. NICK:    Raise your glasses!  Bonnes vacances!

14. JENNY:   Yes!  Here you are, Mum.  Congratulations! Isn't it fantastic?

15. ROY:     I nearly didn't post it, you know.  I can't believe we've won.

16. EILEEN:  You've won, you mean.

17. ROY:     No, You and me - I filled it in for both of us.

1. EILEEN:   Oh, did you!

2. ROY:   (LAUGHS) I had to, the competition was for married couples only.

3.EILEEN:   We don't qualify then.

4.ROY:   Of course we do.  (LAUGHS) Unless I've missed something.  We didn't get divorced, did we?

5.NICK:   I think you'd have noticed, Roy!

6. ROY:   Yes, one of your solicitor friends would have sent me a bloody big bill!

7. EILEEN:   All right we're still married, legally, but we separated six months ago in case you hadn't noticed!

8. JENNY:   Mum.  That doesn't matter for this.

9. EILEEN:   Of course it does, it's for couples and we're not a couple.

10. ROY :   We can pretend, can't we?  (LAUGHS) We have had a bit of practice.

11. NICK:   Yes. Twenty six years of it - should be enough.

A SILENCE

12. EILEEN: (UPSET) Like I said, we don't qualify.

# SCENE 5.

## JENNY AND NICK'S KITCHEN

## JENNY IS UPSET

## F/X: SHE CLUMSILY PUTS PLATES IN THE DISHWASHER.

1. NICK:     Come here, Jenny love.

2. JENNY:    It's crazy. They shouldn't be like that with each other.

3. NICK:     No. But we can't change how your mother feels. The marriage just died  - that's what happens sometimes.

4. JENNY:    Not to my Mum and Dad, it doesn't. If that Michelle hadn't interfered . .

5. NICK:     It wasn't her, it was your mother who made the decision and Eileen isn't the sort to act on impulse, Jenny.

6. JENNY:    (LAUGHS) You're not kidding,  sometimes she can't seem to give you a hug without thinking about it.  She's got to go on this holiday, though.

7. NICK:     She doesn't want to.

8. JENNY:    I'll give her a few days to calm  down then I'll go round and see her.

9. NICK:     OK.

## SCENE 6.

1. ROY:     V/O: Eileen hardly spoke to me when she drove me home after the birthday party - she took the car when we split up and I got to stay in the house - that's the deal so far anyway.

F/X:  DRUM BEAT FAINTLY IN THE

BACKGROUND

I'm not as keen on driving as I used to be anyway - you lose confidence.  Daft when you think I used to drive lorries at one time.  It was good money but I gave it up when our Jenny was born.  It meant Eileen had to go out to work, but I wanted to be at home more, so I could be a real Dad, like mine wasn't.  I liked truck driving.  You felt like you were somebody, sitting up there in that cab, above all the other traffic.

F/X: SWITCHES ON THE TAPE MUSIC:

'TRUCK DRIVING MAN' IN THE

BACKGROUND

(PAUSE) When me and Eileen were in that club in Nashville, she remembered and asked the bloke to sing 'Truck Driving Man'. It's still one of my favourites

F/X: MUSIC TURNED UP LOUDLY

(SINGS) 'Pour me another cup of coffee. It is
the best in the land. Put another nickel in the
juke box, and play 'The Truck Driving Man'. We
used to sing our heads off cruising along the
highways. There's no traffic hardly except in
the cities. We hired this Buick, it had air-
conditioning and cruise control, the lot. It was
a great holiday, till I . . Like Eileen said, I
shouldn't have got so upset. I let things get at
me too much.

## SCENE 7. (F/B 2)

SOUVENIR SHOP IN AMERICA.

F/X:  SHOP DOORBELL RINGS
OCCASIONALLY,  BLUE GRASS MUSIC IN
THE BACKGROUND.

MUSIC:  BLUE GRASS INSTRUMENTAL

1. EILEEN:  Shall we take Nick a cowboy hat back?

2. ROY:  Yeah, why not?  Cause a bit of a stir at the office, won't it?

3. EILEEN:  Do you think he'd wear it?

4. ROY:  I don't know.  How much are they?

5. EILEEN:  Oh, heck, this one's 80 dollars.  We couldn't put it in the suitcase anyway.

6. ROY:  I'll have a look for a book for him.  Or what about a poster?

7. EILEEN:  You mean like the one of that girl wearing six guns and a cowboy hat and very little else?

8. ROY:  Oh, I didn't notice that one.

9. EILEEN:  Not much you didn't!

10.EILEEN:  I think I'll get us one of these miniature rocking chairs.  Or shall I get a wind chime?

F/X:  ROY LOOKING THROUGH A BOOK

1. ROY:      Have you a twenty dollar note, Eileen?  I'm
             going to get this book.

2. EILEEN:   What is it?

3. ROY:      'The Trail of Tears'.  It's the story of the
             Cherokee being driven out by the white man.

4. EILEEN:   What do you want to buy that for?

5. ROY:      I don't know.  (TURNS PAGE) It's that Tsali, I
             want to know about him.  It says here the
             soldiers used to call him Charlie.  Ignorant
             beggars.

6. EILEEN:   I know it was terrible what they did, Roy, but,
             it's only a bit of history.  They put those signs
             up about all sorts.

7. ROY:      Have you got any change?

8. EILEEN:   Yes,  I've got two tens (NOTES PASSED OVER)
             'The Trail of Tears' It's not what I call holiday
             reading.

             <u>F/X: FADE UP DRUM BEAT AND CROSS</u>

             <u>OVER INTO SOUND OF WINDSCREEN</u>

             <u>WIPERS.</u>

## SCENE 8.

F/X: WINDSCREEN WIPERS AND HEAVY
RAIN AS NICK DRIVES HIS CAR
THROUGH RUSH HOUR TRAFFIC.

1. ROY:     I'm glad you spotted me, I'd have got soaked.

2. NICK:    Do you want to come back for tea?

3. ROY:     No, I'm all right, thanks  - unless you want a
            baby-sitter?

4. NICK:    No, I've had to bring some work home with me
            tonight.

5. ROY:     Your boss wanting you to make up for having a
            weekend, is he?

6. NICK:    Something like that.

7. ROY:     It's the way it goes, these days, isn't it?
            Sometimes I think I'd be glad if they did finally
            decide to give me the push.  Men's fashion is for
            the young really.

8. NICK:    Have they said anything lately?

9. ROY:     No.  It's been more relaxed since Mac the Knife
            retired and young Andrew took over.  I trained
            him you know?

10.NICK:    Yes, you said.  He has to be better than his
            predecessor.  I don't think I could have coped
            with working for him.

1. ROY:          Yeah.  Mackenzie took me to hell and back.
                 Just the way he looked at you, as if to say
                 'You're nobody, you'.

                 (PAUSE) I should have stood up to him, I
                 suppose.  But, I'm not exactly hero material.  I
                 wish I was.

2. NICK:         You did well to survive that sort of treatment.
                 You hung on in there, Roy  - that takes some
                 doing, you know.

3. ROY:          (PAUSE) Oh. If you say so.   I suppose it does in
                 a way.

                 <u>F/X: NICK PUTS THE HANDBRAKE ON -</u>
                 <u>READY FOR A LONG WAIT.</u>

4. NICK:         They still haven't fixed these damned traffic
                 lights.

5. ROY:          I wish Andrew could do the appraisals before
                 Christmas, though, get them over with.

6. NICK:         We're glad you've both agreed to come to us for
                 Christmas.

7. ROY:          I hope Eileen's on better terms with me  by
                 then.  How is she?

8. NICK:         Fine.

9. ROY:          It can't be much fun for her, spending dark
                 winter nights on her own, I don't care how cosy
                 that cottage of hers is.

1. NICK:      Not much fun for you either.

2. ROY:       No.  But I'm still coping, and my cooking's improving.  I'm improving all round.  Pity I couldn't have done it sooner, eh?

3. NICK:      It'll come right.

4. ROY:       Do you think Eileen will change her mind about the holiday?

5. NICK:      I don't know.

6. ROY:       No, neither do I.  But I keep hoping.

## SCENE 9.

COTTAGE LIVING ROOM

F/X: WIND RATTLING THE WINDOWS.
EILEEN BOLTS THE DOOR AND PUTS
THE SECURITY CHAIN ACROSS.

1. EILEEN:  V/O: I wish I didn't have an imagination.  I'm all right here on my own at night as long as my imagination doesn't kick in.

Michelle says I ought to get a dog.

I suppose it's an idea.  She's good at ideas is Michelle.

F/X: SHE WALKS AWAY FROM THE
DOOR INTO THE LIVING ROOM.  SHE
SELECTS A CASSETTE.

At least now I can sit and be quiet if I want to, instead of having to listen to Roy going on and on about work, and getting old.

He made such a to-do about being fifty last year - we none of us dared mention it.  I'll get to my big 5 O in July.

SHE PUTS THE TAPE IN THE CASSETTE
PLAYER AND REWINDS THE TAPE.

I think getting old is worse for a woman.  Blokes keep on being blokes somehow, especially where women are concerned!

But for a woman, once she stops looking sexy, well she might as well be invisible.

F/X: PRESSES PLAY

1. EILEEN: V/O: I felt invisible.  Roy just didn't seem to know I was there half the time.

F/X: MUSIC  FADE UP CONCERT INTRO

AND APPLAUSE 'CAN'T SMILE WITHOUT

YOU'  (BARRY MANILOW)

2. EILEEN: V/O:  I like Barry Manilow.  I'd never bothered with him much till Michelle took me and the other girls to that concert.

Listen to me - me and the other girls, they're all at least twenty years younger than me - but I felt I was one of them that night.

F/X:  EILEEN SITS ON THE SOFA.

THE SONG CONTINUES, AND

GRADUALLY FADES INTO THE

BACKGROUND

He picked me out to sing to.  I didn't know where to put myself, but  - the way he looked at me. (PAUSE) I suddenly realised what had been missing for so long.

I'd forgotten what it was like to be looked at like I was somebody really special.

His singing, Barry says, is a gift he has to give - that's why he does it.  (PAUSE)  What have I got to give now I wonder?

There were thousands of us at that concert, and we all felt like sisters, no, better than sisters because there was no rivalry between us , not like me and Janice

22

## SCENE 10.  (F/B 3)

JANICE AND HOWARD'S HOUSE IN
AMERICA.  F/X: PATIO AND SMALL
SWIMMING POOL. CRICKETS. ROY
SWIMMING IN THE POOL.

1. JANICE: Howard usually insists on having the pool drained and covered over by October, but I managed to persuade him to leave it till after your visit.

2. EILEEN: It's fabulous.  Even better than the photos you sent.  I can't get over this place.

3. JANICE: Can't believe your naughty little sister has done so well for herself, can you?

4. EILEEN: Roy's enjoying his swim.

5. JANICE: Yes.  Makes big waves, doesn't he?

6. EILEEN: It's all these breakfasts in diners  - we can't resist them.  Oh, it's great to see you Janice. Ten years is a long time, but you haven't changed much.

7. JANICE: Well, I look after myself.  Nothing else to do is there, as Howard insists I have to be a lady of leisure.

8. EILEEN: You dropped lucky, didn't you?

9. JANICE: Yes, eventually.  (CALLS) Come on out now Roy. Time for cocktails!

F/X:   FADE OUT.  FADE UP AGAIN

COCKTAIL SHAKER, ICE  AND GLASSES.

1. EILEEN:   Aren't we going to wait till Howard gets home?

2. JANICE:   No, he always has a game of golf after work, he'll be ages yet.  Do you play golf, Roy?

3. ROY:   No.  Do you like that CD we got you?

4. JANICE:   Yes, thanks very much.

5. EILEEN:   You always used to pinch my Elvis records.

6. JANICE:   Yeah.  Here's to the bad old days, eh?

7. EILEEN:   (PAUSE)  They weren't that bad.

8. JANICE;   Pity you don't play golf, Roy, we were hoping to get rid of both you and Howard at the same time.  Isn't that right, Eileen?

9. EILEEN:   (LAUGHS) Yeah.

10.JANICE:   I think all men should have a hobby, don't you? (LAUGHS)  Something to keep their hands occupied.

### EILEEN LAUGHS.

11.ROY:   I've got a hobby, it's called going to work.

12.JANICE:   Where are you working now?  I lose track of you and your jobs.

1. EILEEN:   Roy moved into the men's fashion business.

2. JANICE:   Oh. Doing what?

3. EILEEN:   I'm still in the admin at the university.  Is Howard still in the same job?

4. JANICE:   No.  He's just gone up in the world actually, they've made him a partner.  We're taking you out to a swish restaurant tomorrow to celebrate.

5. EILEEN: Oh, I don't think we've got the right clothes with us for that.

6. JANICE: Don't worry, Howard said I can take you to the Mall and buy whatever you need for your visit with us.

7. EILEEN; We can't let you do that.

8. JANICE: Don't bother arguing, Eileen. You stopped me doing what I wanted when I was little, but you've no chance now. If I wanna treat ya, honey, I'm gonna treat ya!.

9. ROY: Oh, I like the accent, Janice.

10, JANICE: Don't tell Howard. He goes mad if he hears me talking like that, he likes me to stay the little English girl he married.

11. EILEEN: Does he always get what he wants?

12. JANICE: Only if it suits me. You don't let Roy have all his own way, do you?

13. EILEEN: Of course not!

## SCENE 11.

ROY'S KITCHEN.

F/X: ONION BEING CHOPPED. ELVIS
TAPE PLAYING IN THE BACKGROUND
MUSIC: US MAIL   (ELVIS PRESLEY)

1. ROY:    V/O: I'm doing Cajun Chicken tonight, one of
my specialities.  I make enough for two and
freeze one.  I've got quite interested in cooking.

We ate steak and chicken nearly all the time in
America.  At Janice's it was all barbecue and
micro-wave.

We bought this Elvis tape at the Country Music
Hall of Fame in Nashville.  It's the one we got for
Janice as well.

Janice didn't want to hear about Nashville, or
any of our holiday really.  She just wanted to
talk about her and Howard and money.   Apart
from golf, that seems to be Howard's main
interest, money.

He was generous, though, I'll give him that.  Too
generous, if you know what I mean, especially
when it could get noticed.

And then there was Janice and Eileen being 'all
girls together', and having a dig at men all the
time.  Mostly me, because Howard was at work.

I used to go off on my own when I could. I read
my book, and did a lot of thinking.  Too much
perhaps.

I'm looking forward to Christmas - and a chance
to talk to Eileen.

## SCENE 12.

F/X: SHOPPING CENTRE.. CROWDS..
CAROLS PLAYED OVER LOUDSPEAKER
SYSTEMS.

MUSIC:  CAROLS

(CHOIR OF KING'S COLLEGE
CAMBRIDGE)

1. EILEEN:   It's a quarter to twelve.  Shall we go in here for some lunch before it gets too crowded.

2. JENNY:   Oh, yes, I'm desperate to have a sit down.

3. EILEEN:   I told you you should have left the Christmas shopping to me and Nick.

4. JENNY:   I just wanted to get Nick's present.  Even though it's his money I'm buying it with.

5. EILEEN:   Oh, don't start worrying about his money and your money - that only leads to trouble.

6. JENNY:   The voice of experience, eh?

7. EILEEN:   Come on, let's get in here and find a table.

## SCENE 13.

### TEA ROOM.

### F/X: CHRISTMAS CAROLS FILTER THROUGH FROM THE SHOPPING CENTRE.

1. EILEEN: I like their decorations. I've not done anything much at the cottage, didn't seem worth it as I'll be at your place.

2. JENNY: Dad hasn't bothered either. He's really looking forward to coming for Christmas though.

3. EILEEN: So am I. Are you sure you won't let me cook the turkey?

4. JENNY: Yes, Nick's persuaded me to give in and take you up on the offer.

5. EILEEN: Good. You put your feet up as much as possible.

6. JENNY: Actually, I'd like another favour, I feel a bit cheeky asking . .

7. EILEEN: Go on.

8. JENNY: Nick and I have been invited to a party on Boxing Night, would you babysit?

9. EILEEN: Of course I will.

10. JENNY: Reckon you can cope with being on your own with Dad, do you?

11.EILEEN: Oh.

1. JENNY: He still loves you, you know.

2. EILEEN: He has a funny way of showing it.

3. JENNY: What have you bought him for Christmas - a year's subscription to Loaded, to make him feel young again?

4. EILEEN; I've bought him a polo shirt.

5. JENNY: Oh, for the holiday?

6. EILEEN: No.

7. JENNY: But you are going, aren't you?

8. EILEEN: I haven't made my mind up.

9. JENNY: Are you disappointed it's the South of France and not the cruise?

10.EILEEN: No. I knew what we'd win after your Dad told me which photo he'd sent them. Him and me in our jeans in front of a giant plastic pumpkin, I ask you!

11.JENNY: He thought it was a lovely one of you.

12.EILEEN: Yes, but, it wasn't exactly glamorous. And it was obvious they'd use the photos to decide who got which prize. They'd have decided who'd look best at the captain's table, who'd look best in a bikini, and who'd make a couple of good clowns at the Carnival.

13.JENNY: It's still a wonderful holiday, and all expenses paid. You'd be crazy to turn it down.

14. EILEEN: Yes, I know. But if I go, he'll think I want us to get back together.

15. JENNY: Don't you?

3. EILEEN: Look, Jenny, I know you think I shouldn't have walked out like I did, but I had good cause. He was so miserable and I couldn't get through to him, however much I tried.

4. JENNY: I know. But do you really want to live the rest of your life on your own in that cottage?

5. EILEEN: I'm not on my own all the time. Michelle and the girls come round.

6. JENNY: Do they? I thought Michelle was all tied up with this new boyfriend of hers.

7. EILEEN: Look, Jenny I'm all right as I am. And I'm enjoying being able to please myself, like I can have what I want to eat instead of him sulking if I didn't make him his favourites.

8. JENNY: He wanted a bit of fuss, that's all.

9. EILEEN: So did I, but I didn't get it. Even when I got a promotion instead of the sack.

10.JENNY: If you were back together, you could sell the cottage and spend Grandad's money on holidays and all sorts.

11. EILEEN: We could have done that in the first place, if he hadn't been so stupid about it being my Dad's money.

12. JENNY: It wasn't just you having more money, it was work and everything else.

13. EILEEN: All I did was buy him a watch for an anniversary present, to try to .. .. - and look where it got me.

EILEEN IS UPSET..

1. JENNY:     (LIGHT)  Yeah, you bought him a gold watch
              and he got you a pair of secateurs and
              gardening gloves.

2. EILEEN:    Why did it have to be something practical?  I
              know I'm the practical sort, Jenny, I've had to
              be.  But could he not, just for once, have bought
              me a bunch of flowers?

## **SCENE 14.**

ROY'S LIVING ROOM.

F/X: ROY SETS UP THE IRONING
BOARD   CD PLAYING: 'SEA OF
HEARTBREAK' (DON GIBSON)

1. ROY:   V/O: I hate ironing.  I usually don't bother
ironing my casual shirts, but I don't want to
look a mess.

ROY IRONS AND SINGS LOUDLY

'Memories of your caress.  Love divine. How I
wish that you were mine - again my dear, no
more sea of tears, sea of heartbreak.'

F/X: TRACK ENDS, CD OFF.

I've bought Eileen some perfume for Christmas.
Jennifer told me which sort to get.

It's the little things that send your life the wrong
way.   Like buying somebody the wrong
present, or saying the wrong thing.

I'd had enough of watching what I said at work,
and Eileen lost patience with me and my
worrying. Like she said, you can only take so
much.

I know what happened to me was nothing like
what Tsali went through, but . . .

We both stopped talking about work in the end,
we stopped talking about anything. (PAUSE) I
hope she talks to me at Christmas.

## SCENE 15.

NICK AND JENNY'S KITCHEN.

F/X: MUSIC HEARD FAINTLY FROM THE
LOUNGE

MUSIC:   'HAVE YOURSELF A MERRY
LITTLE CHRISTMAS' (ELLA FITZGERALD)

F/X:  CUTLERY, CROCKERY, BREAD
UNWRAPPED ETC

1. JENNY:     Don't put stuffing on all the sandwiches, Mum,
             Nick's not all that keen on stuffing.

2. EILEEN:    I thought you wanted to watch that film with
             your Dad?

3. NICK:      Yes, will you go and sit down!  Your mother and
             I can cope.

4. JENNY:     O.K. I'll leave you to it.  Thanks.(EXITS)

5. EILEEN:    That baby'll be born running around.  Have you
             decided on a name yet?

6. NICK:      No.

7. EILEEN:    It's something you have to be very careful about,
             names.  You make the tea, I'll do the
             sandwiches.  Would you like tomato on yours?

8. NICK:      Yes, please.

F/X: KETTLE, TOMATOES ETC.

1. EILEEN: Roy's parents were very ambitious for him, him being their only child. They chose Roy because it meant 'the king'. So does Rex - it's a wonder his mother didn't call him that and get him a collar and lead to go with it.

2. NICK: (LAUGHS) Yes, I gather she was a force to be reckoned with.

3. EILEEN: A bully, you mean. It's a wonder Roy survived the way he did really.

4. NICK: He's very good company.

5. EILEEN: Yes, he's always been one for a laugh. He used to say that's why I married him - for a laugh. I like a bit of fun, but I need somebody else to start me off. I'm inclined to get too serious sometimes.

6. NICK: It's a serious business, looking after a family.

7. EILEEN: Yes. The worst thing for me was having to go out to work when Jenny was little. Still, it couldn't be helped.

8. ROY: (ENTERS) Am I allowed another beer?

9. EILEEN: I can see I'll be baby-sitting on my own tonight, Nick. He'll be flat out on the sofa.

10. ROY: I won't!

11. NICK: Are you two arguing again?

1. EILEEN:   No, not really.

2. ROY:   We're doing better than last Christmas when I had Michelle the Man-Hater to cope with as well as Eileen. Talk about being got at!

3. EILEEN:   She'd just got divorced.

4. ROY:   Yeah, but she didn't have to take it out on me!

5. EILEEN:   She's over all that now. She was even saying nice things about you the other day.

6. ROY:   I don't believe it.

7. EILEEN:   She was saying that at least you'd been faithful, stuck to one sweetie instead of going for the whole pick and mix like her husband did.

8. ROY:   Oh.

9. NICK:   There you are Roy, put that on your CV, 'faithful and trustworthy'. What do you think, Eileen, have you anything to add to that?

10. EILEEN:   Yes - 'and good for a laugh'.

11. ROY:   I think I'll go and drink this beer while I decide how to take that. (EXITS)

### F/X: PLATES, CUPS ETC

12. EILEEN:   He won't want a cup of tea now.

1. NICK:      So Michelle thinks Roy's OK after all, does she?

2. EILEEN:  Yes.

3. NICK:      Bit of a change of heart.

4. EILEEN:  (PAUSE) Yes.  But she was very kind to me when me and Roy, were having our difficulties.

5. NICK:      Yes.

6. EILEEN:  I don't know where I'd have gone if she hadn't let me stay at her flat.

7. NICK:      Back to Roy?

<u>A SILENCE</u>

8. EILEEN:  It all happened a bit quick, really, didn't it?  Perhaps I should have taken a bit longer to think about it.  (PAUSE) But like my mother used to say, if you make mistakes you have to live with them.

9. NICK:      Do you?  Why?

# SCENE 16.

## NICK AND JENNY'S LOUNGE

1. EILEEN: V/O: It was strange, the two of us sitting in the lounge on our own, watching tele together like we used to. I like watching television, me and my Mum used to watch it a lot after I'd put our Janice to bed.

Some of the programmes are rubbish, of course, but I like a nice film or a good discussion. There was this programme a few weeks ago, they were going on about how men aren't good at talking about things.

Roy's never been very good with words, but I used to wish he'd at least try.

It's not much to ask for, is it, a few kind words?

(PAUSE)

It could have made all the difference, a few kind words.

2. ROY: Here you are, love, one Bailey's with ice. And this. It's just a little extra present.

F/X: SMALL PRESENT HANDED OVER

3. EILEEN: Oh, a CD.

4. ROY: How did you guess? I meant to give it to you before, but I forgot where I'd put it.

F/X: CD UNWRAPPED

5. EILEEN: Shania Twain.

1. ROY:     She was the one who had that big hit when we
            were in America.

2. EILEEN:  Yes.

3. ROY:     It has some nice songs on it.  Good words to
            them.

4. EILEEN:  Thanks very much.  Did you choose it?

5. ROY:     Of course I did.

6. EILEEN:  You mean you thought it up all on your own
            and went out and bought it.  My goodness!

7. ROY:     All right.

8. EILEEN:  Sorry.  Thanks very much.

                    (PAUSE)

9. ROY:     Eileen, about the holiday.  The thing is, we have
            to let them know by next week what date we
            want to go.  I mean if we're going.

10.EILEEN:  Oh.

11.ROY:     It'd be quite an experience, wouldn't it, Nice and
            the Cote d'Azur.

12.EILEEN:  Yes.

13.ROY:     Apparently it's like summertime there in
            February, that's how they can have all these
            flower parades and that.

14.EILEEN:  Yes, it must be lovely.

1.ROY:      Won't you come?

### A SILENCE

2. ROY:     I just want to go on this holiday with you.  Just
            to spend some time together.

3. EILEEN:  Would we have to share a room?

4. ROY:     Oh, I expect so. (TRIES TO LAUGH) But, it's not
            as if we'd be seeing anything we hadn't seen
            before, is it?

5. EILEEN:  (PAUSE)  No.

6. ROY:     Please, Eileen. No strings, I just want you to
            share it with me.  I don't want to go on my own.

7. EILEEN:  Perhaps they wouldn't let you anyway.

8. ROY:     No.

9. EILEEN:  Our Jennifer's determined we should go.  And
            Nick seems to think we should as well.

10.ROY:     We might never get a chance like this again.

11.EILEEN:  No.

12.ROY:     Now or never, eh?

# SCENE 17.

F/X: ROY'S GARDEN. BIRDS.

ROY IS RAKING UP LEAVES

NICK APPROACHES PUSHING DANIEL IN HIS PRAM.

1. NICK:     Have you got time for a visitor?

2. ROY:      (LOUDLY) Oh, hello Nick!  Oh, sorry, is he asleep?

3. NICK:     Yes, that was the idea.  I'll park him inside the greenhouse.

4. ROY:      We can go in the house if you want.

5. NICK:     (MOVING AWAY WITH THE PUSHCHAIR)  No, I'm enjoying the fresh air.

6. ROY:      So am I.

F/X: ROY CARRIES ON RAKING THE LEAVES

7. NICK:     (APPROACHING)  I brought him out to give Jenny a chance to rest,  she gets very tired at the moment.

8. ROY:      (STOPS RAKING)  But she's all right?

9. NICK:     Oh, yes.  Just a bit worried about how much weight she's put on already.

10.ROY:      Women are daft like that.  Eileen tries to remember to walk around with her nose in the air, so no-one will notice her double chin. Makes me laugh.

<u>F/X:  RAKES THE LEAVES AGAIN</u>

1. NICK:     I wish my garden were as well looked after as yours.

2. ROY:      I just thought I'd better have it tidy  in case Eileen comes round.

3. NICK:     Oh, are you expecting her?

4. ROY:      No.  But she has phoned me a couple of times, about the holiday arrangements. (RAKES LEAVES AGAIN)  She always did most of the gardening as well as . . . . you never realise . . .

5. NICK:     No.  I've brought a couple of beers, thought we could celebrate your appraisal.

6. ROY:      Oh, Jenny told you, did she?  Shall we sit on the bench, I could do with a rest.

<u>F/X:  BEER CANS OPENED</u>

7. ROY:      I wanted to tell Eileen I'd done well, but Jenny says to save it till the right moment, when we're together on our own on the holiday.

8. NICK:     Yes, not long now.

9. ROY:      I've had a phone call from this journalist from the magazine, Samantha Dalton she's called. Sounds very professional.  And she's sent me a few more details.  Do you want to have a look?

<u>F/X: HE TAKES A CRUMPLED LEAFLET</u>

<u>OUT OF HIS POCKET</u>

1. ROY:     Sorry, it's got a bit creased in my pocket.  Off to
            the South of France next week, not bad, eh!

PAUSE AS NICK READS

2. NICK:    Have you shown this to Eileen?

3. ROY:     No.

4. NICK:    What exactly have you told her about this
            holiday you've won?

5. ROY:     That it's a week at a four star hotel in Nice.

6. NICK:    And have you told her this other 'small detail'?

7. ROY:     What?

8. NICK;    That it's a second honeymoon.

9. ROY:     No.  No, I haven't told her that bit.

## SCENE 18.

EILEEN'S BEDROOM

F/X: EILEEN PACKING HER CASE -
COATHANGERS, TISSUE PAPER. TAPE
PLAYING IN THE BACKGROUND.

MUSIC: WHEN WE DON'T TALK (SHANIA
TWAIN)

1. EILEEN: V/O I always take too many clothes with me when I go away. I'm never sure what to wear.

I'm only going to please our Jennifer. Though I have to admit I'm looking forward to a holiday.

The girls at work think it's hilarious, me having to share a bedroom with Roy like this.

They're sex mad. They talk about the lot. They took me to one of those underwear and god knows what parties the other week. I didn't know where to look.

I hadn't been out with them for ages. (PAUSE) Michelle and the girls were very helpful when I was looking for somewhere to live. Mind you, I couldn't have bought anything without my Dad's money

Everyone likes the idea of a new home, don't they? But when we'd all got over the excitement of buying the cottage and the curtains and everything - well, it's awkward for them really, me being that much older. We have a different outlook on life.

(CONTINUED)

1. EILEEN:   They make such a fuss about sex, don't they, these days.

(PAUSE)

I've bought a new nightie for Nice, from Marks and Spencer's.

## **SCENE 19.**

### F/X: CABIN OF A PLANE IN MID AIR.

1. PILOT: Ladies and gentlemen, we are about to fly over Paris.  Our estimated time of arrival at Nice airport is 1400 hours.

2. ROY: Ooh, look there's the river Seine.  Where's the Eiffel Tower?

3. EILEEN: Careful, you nearly knocked my drink over!

4. ROY: Flying over Paris with a glass of champagne in your hand  - isn't it fantastic!

5. EILEEN: Yeah.

6. ROY: And all because I filled in a competition.  Aren't you glad you know me?

7. EILEEN: I wouldn't go so far as to say that.

8. ROY: Oh, go on - force yourself!

9. EILEEN: (LAUGHS) Pour me some more champagne and I'll think about it.

### F/X: CHAMPAGNE POURED

10. ROY: I hope they bring us our dinner soon.

11. EILEEN: So do I,  or I'll be tiddly.

12. ROY: We're going to have a great time, aren't we?

1. EILEEN: Yes. Oh, I've always wanted to do this, the South of France, sunshine and flowers in February.

2. ROY: Staying in a top hotel!

3. EILEEN: I'm looking forward to a trip along the coast to Monaco.

4. ROY: Monte Carlo, you mean. We'll have to send your Janice a postcard from there. Do you think she'll be impressed, us flying first class and everything?

5. EILEEN: Does it matter?

6. ROY: Yes, it does.

<u>A SILENCE</u>

7. EILEEN: That's the trouble with you, you never forget anything.

8. ROY: You didn't forget anything either. You left nothing out, did you! You took me apart, you and Janice.

9. EILEEN: We didn't. We were only joking.

10. ROY: Yeah! Like you and Michelle used to.

11. EILEEN: You seem to forget we couldn't have afforded that holiday without Janice getting us those cheap flights and having us to stay.

12. ROY: Oh, we're back to me having to be grateful, are we!

1. EILEEN:   What do you mean?

2. ROY:   You always seem to think I should be grateful - for everything.

3. EILEEN:   What do you mean?

4. ROY:   Never mind.

5. EILEEN:   Oh, you're not going to go in one of your moods this holiday as well, are you?  I'll begin to wish I hadn't come.

6. ROY:   And I might begin to wish I hadn't asked you.  I got you this holiday, and you haven't even bothered to say thank you properly.

7 EILEEN:   Keep your voice down!  They're coming with the food!  Perhaps you'll be in a better mood when you've had something to eat!

8. EILEEN:   V/O:  It'll spoil everything if he goes back to being moody like he was on the last holiday.  I suppose he had cause in a way.  Janice always was a torment, and I let her.  But he kept going on about the Cherokees, and, well, it was embarrassing, Howard being an American.

## SCENE 20.

HOTEL FOYER

F/X: GUESTS. BACKGROUND
MUSIC.MUSIC:  OSCAR PETERSON OR
FRANCOISE HARDY

1. SAMANTHA: Samantha Dalton, 'Que Sera' magazine.  So
pleased to meet you, Roy, and Eileen.  Sorry I
wasn't at the airport, but I trust the chauffeur
took care of you.

(TOGETHER)

2. EILEEN:  Yes.  Hello.

3. ROY:  Oh, hello, Miss Dalton.  Yes, thanks, he met us
O K.

4. SAMANTHA:  Please, it's Samantha.  Now what do you
think of Nice?

5. ROY:  Oh, it looks lovely.

6. SAMANTHA:  And are you impressed with the hotel?

7. ROY:  Oh, yes, very swish.

8. SAMANTHA:  Wait till you see your room, Eileen, it's
superb.  I'll get them to take you up later, but
first of all, if you don't mind I'd like a couple of
photos of you arriving.

9. EILEEN:  Now?  I'll need to comb my hair.

10.SAMANTHA: It won't take a minute, I just want you at the
hotel entrance, under the palm trees on the
Promenade des Anglais.  Come on, Eileen,
quickly, it doesn't matter about your hair.

## SCENE 21.

### F/X: THE PROMENADE DES ANGLAIS
### TRAFFIC, SEA, TOURISTS.

1. EILEEN:  Oh, isn't it lovely.  Oh, I hope our bedroom is one with a sea view.

2. SAMANTHA: Yes, don't worry you've got a balcony.  Now stand there, looking out across the sea. Good.

### F/X:  CAMERA SOUND AS SEVERAL
### SHOTS ARE TAKEN.

3. SAMANTHA: OK.  That's it for now.  I'm just going off to take some more shots of the Promenade and the beach.  I'll see you at the reception this evening.

4. EILEEN:  Oh, is there a reception?

5. SAMANTHA: Just a small buffet and glass of champagne to toast your arrival, and a few photos for the local tourist board.  We have a promotional agreement with them.

6. EILEEN:  Oh.  What do you want us to wear?

7. SAMANTHA: Something smart - if you can.

8. EILEEN:  (IRRITATED) We'll do our best.

9. SAMANTHA: See you later, then.  I'll ask Christophe to keep an eye on you. He's the reception and bar assistant.  He speaks very good English.

1. ROY:       Oh, that's good.  See you at the reception then.

2. EILEEN:    I hope we're not going to be stuck with her all
              week, bossing us about.

3. ROY:       We have to do stuff for the magazine, it's part of
              the deal.

4. EILEEN:    I suppose so.  Oh, look at it, palm trees and
              pansies everywhere.

5. ROY:       Shall we walk along a bit before we go back to
              the hotel?

6. EILEEN:    Yes, all right.

7. ROY:       We'd better walk arm in arm, in case she's
              watching.  We're supposed to be a couple,
              remember.

8. EILEEN:    Oh, yes.  All right then.

9. ROY:       V/O:  It was the first time I'd been so close to
              her for a long time.  You can get out of the
              habit, can't you, you know, touching each other.

              When things started to go wrong, it sounds daft,
              it got that I felt as if I didn't dare touch her - I
              was getting enough put-downs from Mackenzie
              without asking for any more.

              (LAUGHS) And anyway, she seemed more
              bothered about that Barry Manilow than me.
              Call that singing? I could give him a run for his
              money any day!

## SCENE 22.

HOTEL BEDROOM:  F/X: THE PORTER
PUTS THE SUITCASES ON LUGGAGE
RACK

1. PORTER: J'ouvre les volets, oui?

2. ROY:      (PAUSE) Oh, the shutters, yes please.

F/X:  WINDOWS AND SHUTTERS
OPENED.  DISTANT TRAFFIC AND
SEAGULLS

3. PORTER: That will be all, Monsieur?

4. ROY:      Yes.  Thanks very much.  Oh.

F/X: ROY GIVES HIM A TIP.

5. PORTER: Merci, monsieur.

F/X: DOOR CLOSED

6. ROY:      I gave him ten francs. do you think that was
            enough?  He didn't look very pleased.   Eileen?

A SILENCE

7. EILEEN;  I thought it would be twin beds.

8. ROY:      Oh.  Fantastic room, though, isn't it?

9. EILEEN:  Yes.  We'd better unpack, and then go and look
            for somewhere to get a bit of something to eat.

1. ROY: There'll be food at the reception, Christophe said.

2. EILEEN: That's not till seven and it'll only be nibbles. - I don't want you starving and showing me up, grabbing at it two-handed.

3. ROY: Right.

4. EILEEN: (PAUSE) Do you want me to make us a cup of tea now - there's all the stuff here.

5. ROY: Yes, that'd be nice.

F/X: EILEEN FILLS THE KETTLE SETS OUT CUPS

F/X: SUITCASE OPENED . SOUND OF COATHANGERS ETC AS ROY UNPACKS HIS CLOTHES

6. ROY: The last time we were in a hotel was in America.

7. EILEEN: Yes.

8. ROY: It was a great holiday that - I've been thinking about it a lot lately.

9. EILEEN: Have you?

10. ROY: Yeah, I watched the video again a few weeks ago, and it's done me a lot of good.

11. EILEEN: How do you mean?

12. ROY: Well, do you remember that guy who made you those pancakes?

1. EILEEN:   Oh, yes, he was lovely.

2. ROY:   He said he was the best pancake maker in Virginia.

3. EILEEN;   Yes?

4. ROY:   That's what's so great about Americans, they believe they can be somebody - it's the American dream - they can make it in some way. Be a success.

5. EILEEN:   Is all this leading somewhere, because the tea's ready.

6. ROY:   I've been trying to be like that bloke. It's made me do better at the job, and, I'm much happier at work now.

7. EILEEN:   Oh. Better late than never I suppose.

8. ROY:   Yeah. Well, I just wanted you to know. (PAUSE) You and me were really up against it, weren't we, what with your job and my job?

9. EILEEN:   (PAUSE) Do you still take sugar?

10. ROY:   Yes.

## SCENE 23.

HOTEL, SMALL  RECEPTION ROOM

F/X: PEOPLE CHATTING, CHAMPAGNE
POURED.

1. ROY:       The champagne still seems to be flowing, do you
              want some more?

2. EILEEN:    No. Why didn't you tell me?

3. ROY:       Tell you what?

4. EILEEN:    You know what!  About it being a second
              honeymoon!

5. ROY:       I didn't think it mattered.

6. EILEEN:    Of course it matters.  No wonder it wasn't twin
              beds.  Have you seen what it says in this
              publicity hand-out they've done?

7. ROY:       Oh, is it in English as well as French?

8. EILEEN:    Yes. (READS) Que Sera' magazine is giving three
              couples a second honeymoon, an opportunity to
              put the romance back into their marriage and to
              recapture the passion of their wedding night!'

9. SAMANTHA: And I'll be there with my new camera!  Are
              you enjoying yourselves?

10. ROY:      Oh, yes, thanks.

1. SAMANTHA: I must take some photos of you in the bridal suite, but I'll leave it till later. The dining room is just through there. Do you mind if I don't join you for dinner? I have to see someone.

2. EILEEN: No, we don't mind at all.

3. ROY: A candlelit dinner for two, is it, Samantha?

4. SAMANTHA: What else on your honeymoon?

5. EILEEN: It's not really a honeymoon, though, is it?

6. SAMANTHA: Of course it is, that's why we need the bedroom photos et cetera, as we agreed on the phone, Roy.

7. ROY: Yes.

8. SAMANTHA: See you in the morning.

9. ROY: Yes, goodnight.

10.EILEEN: And you agreed to it all, did you, this second honeymoon bit?

12.ROY: Yes.

13.EILEEN: And you kept it quiet.

14.ROY: I thought you might not come if you knew.

15.EILEEN: Too right I wouldn't.

16. ROY: Shall we go in for dinner now?

17. EILEEN: Yes, and after dinner we'll go straight upstairs and sort that bed out.

3. ROY:        What do you mean?

4. EILEEN:    It's two singles zipped together.  So we'll just go and unzip them and push them apart, shall we!

5. ROY:        (PAUSE) If that's what you want.

6. EILEEN:    V/O:  I know I shouldn't have been like that with him.  It was that Samantha that had upset me, she made me so mad, but there was no need for me to take it out on Roy.

                 I don't know what she wrote down about us. She was more interested in giving 'the come on' to that good looking assistant manager.

                 She wasn't even listening properly to what we were saying.

                 <u>(PAUSE)</u>

                 I'm not very good at listening sometimes.  When Roy kept trying to explain to me about Tsali and why it had upset him so much, I . . well, you can't change what's already happened, can you?

# SCENE 24.

HOTEL BEDROOM

F/X:  ROY IS SNORING GENTLY.

THE TELEPHONE RINGS.

1. ROY:        (WAKING UP)  Hello? . . .Oh, Good morning, Samantha. Now?  Can't it wait till later?  Oh. Right.  Yes.

F/X: HE PUTS DOWN THE RECEIVER

2. ROY:        Eileen.  Eileen, love, wake up.

3. EILEEN:     What?

4. ROY:        Wake up, Samantha's coming to photograph us in bed.

5. EILEEN:     What?

6. ROY:        She'll be up her in about ten minutes.

7. EILEEN:     Oh, for heaven's sake.

8. ROY:        We'll have to be quick.  We'll have to put the bed back together or she'll know, we,   I mean, she'll expect . . .

9. EILEEN:     Oh, my God!  Quick, get the sheets off!

1.ROY:        V/O: Samantha said she had had her orders from her editor.  She had to get  some sexy photos of me and Eileen 'relaxing' in the bridal suite.

It was dead embarrassing.

She made Eileen sort of recline against me. She'd brought this negligee thing with her and made Eileen change into it.

I was sweating a bit, wondering what she was going to make me do.

(PAUSE)

At one time me and Eileen would have had a good laugh about something like that.

## SCENE 25.

F/X: FADE

UP THE SOUNDS OF NICE, THE OLD
TOWN  SEAGULLS, NARROW STREETS
OF FOUR STOREY HOUSES. STREET
EVENTUALLY LEADS TO A MARKET.
PASSERS BY SPEAKING FRENCH,
ENGLISH AND GERMAN. SHOPKEEPERS
CALLING OUT IN SHOPS OPEN TO THE
STREET.

1. EILEEN:   V/O: It's so beautiful here.  They have whole
flower beds full of cyclamen.

This is the old part of Nice.  I love it -  these tall
narrow houses and shops are sort of squeezing
together shoulder to shoulder.

And they've got green shutters and lovely little
balconies.  And the colours!  Yellow, and pink,
and that browny gold colour.

And it's so warm, like a summer's day, in
February.  You can't help but be happy.

2. SAMANTHA: Right the flower Market's at the other end of
this street.  I'll take a couple of photos on the
way.  Please, don't wander off this time, Roy.

F/X: THEY WALK ALONG A NARROW
STREET.

1. SAMANTHA; Now, Eileen, if we could have a shot of you looking at those leather handbags. Our readers love to see someone getting a bargain.

2. ROY: Do you want me in this one as well?

4. SAMANTHA: No, just Eileen. A bit more to the left. Do you think you could take your cardigan off?

4. EILEEN: Yes, O. K.

5. SAMANTHA: Actually, I've brought this gorgeous scarf along, to brighten up your outfit a little. Would you mind?

6. EILEEN: All right, but can we go for a drink soon?

7. SAMANTHA: Yes, don't worry, I want you in a café in the Market square, so you can have a drink there. Now stand still. Oh. How about if you look upwards, look up at the bags near the top of the stand - yes, that's better.

## SCENE 26.

> F/X:  MARKET SQUARE WITH CAFES AROUND THE EDGE, FLOWER MARKET IN THE CENTRE. STALL HOLDERS, SHOPPERS, TOURISTS.
>
> ROY, EILEEN AND SAMANTHA ARE SITTING AT A TABLE IN A STREET CAFÉ. BOTTLES AND GLASSES AS DRINKS ARE POURED.  A STREET MUSICIAN NEARBY PLAYING 'LA VIE EN ROSE' ON ACOUSTIC GUITAR.

1. EILEEN:   Look at the azaleas they're bringing to that stall.

2. SAMANTHA: Keep still,  Eileen!  We can't go to the flower Market until I've got some decent café photos.

> F/X:  CAMERA SHUTTER

3. ROY:       (MOUTH HALF FULL) Lovely ham sandwich.

> F/X:   CAMERA SHUTTERM THEN SAMANTHA SITS DOWN AND TAKES OUT NOTEBOOK AND PEN.

4. SAMANTHA: You seem to like flowers, Eileen.  Are you a keen gardener?

5. EILEEN:   Yes, I am, when I have the time.

6. SAMANTHA: (WRITES NOTE) Good, that will tie in with the flower Market.  Do you have a large garden?

> (SIMULTANEOUS)

1. EILEEN:    No, not now.

2. ROY:       Yes, pretty big.

3. SAMANTHA:  Which is it?

4. ROY:       Eileen means we used to have a bigger garden in our previous house.

5. SAMANTHA:  (MAKING NOTES) Right. And what kind of house do you live in now?

6. ROY:       That guitar player's very good, isn't he? My father used to sing this song, 'La Vie en Rose', isn't it?

7. SAMANTHA:  Yes. Was your father a singer?

8. ROY:       No, but he used to sing this as his party piece, in French when he wanted to show off.

9. EILEEN:    Which was most of the time.

10. SAMANTHA: Oh, can you sing, Roy?

11. ROY:      No.

12. EILEEN:   Yes, you can.

13. SAMANTHA: We can have one of you singing with the guitarist. They're always happy to pose for a few francs.

14. ROY:      No. Is there a gents toilet in here?

1.SAMANTHA:  Yes, inside the café at the far end.

2. ROY:      Right.

### F/X:  CHAIR SCRAPES AS HE EXITS

3. EILEEN:   He wanted to be a singer at one time, but his Dad wouldn't have liked the  competition.

4. SAMANTHA: He shouldn't have let that stop him.

I never let my father stop me.  Go for what you want, that's what I say.

5. EILEEN:   Yes,  but sometimes it's not what you do want, in the end.. .

6. SAMANTHA: Have you anything a bit more spicy for the personal story angle?

7. EILEEN:   Oh.

8. SAMANTHA: Our readers like a bit of drama.  Adultery's their favourite of course, but that won't apply here, will it?

9. EILEEN;   No.

10.SAMANTHA: The stories we get.  It must be nice to get to your age and not have to worry about sex any more.

11.EILEEN:  If you say so.

12.SAMANTHA: I don't know why there are so many problems, I mean, it's no big deal, not much to ask, is it really, going to bed with someone?

13.EILEEN:  I suppose not, if you love them.

14. SAMANTHA:    Hell, we're behind schedule.  We must get the flower Market done before twelve.

## SCENE 27.

F/X: THE FLOWER MARKET.  SHOPPERS,
STALL HOLDERS ETC  BARREL ORGAN
IN THE DISTANCE.

1.EILEEN:     Oh, the scent of those lilies and freesias.  Look
              at those beautiful bouquets.  Oh.

2. SAMANTHA: Can I have you in front of those gladioli and
             the sprays of mimosa?

             You hold this bunch of red roses, Roy and put
             your arm round her.  Well, smile at him, Eileen.
             Hold it!

             F/X  CAMERA SHUTTER CLOSES
             SEVERAL TIMES

3. SAMANTHA: Now give her a kiss. Go on!

             F/X:  CAMERA AGAIN

4. EILEEN:   V/O I hadn't had his arms round me for so long
             that I'd almost forgotten what it felt like, having
             him so close.   (PAUSE) I felt a bit of a flutter
             inside like I used to with him.  I hadn't felt like
             that for years.

             I don't mean that we hadn't slept together but,
             you know how it is, you go along with it but
             your mind's often elsewhere

             PAUSE

1. EILEEN:  V/O: There was a mirror behind one of the stalls. We walked back through the Market after he'd kissed me and I looked in this mirror.

And for the first time for ages my reflection didn't drag me down, I looked quite bonny.

Of course it could have been the light  - artists came to the South of France for the light, didn't they?

## **SCENE 28.**

### F/X: TRAIN ALONG THE COAST

1. EILEEN: It was easy, wasn't it - un aller et retour, and here we are!  And there's plenty of trains back.

2. ROY: Samantha won't be very pleased when she finds out we've gone to Monaco without her.  She wanted to feature Monte Carlo.

3. EILEEN: Christophe will give her a drink and calm her down.

4. ROY: Yeah.  He's a nice lad.

5. EILEEN: Yes.  Oh, it's lovely to go somewhere on our own.

6. ROY: Yeah.  Just the two of us.

## SCENE 29.

MONACO HARBOUR.

F/X:  GENTLE WAVES, CLINK OF SAIL
FASTENINGS, SEAGULLS. DISTANT
TRAFFIC. DRUMS FAINTLY IN THE
BACKGROUND

1. ROY:      V/O: On the Riviera they have harbours full of
yachts like we have car parks full of cars.
There's a really big white cruiser over there, it
must be Prince Rainier's.

His palace is right up on top of the cliff.  Must
be great to be somebody like that, to have your
own little kingdom, your own people.

Like Tsali, he had his own people.  He's a legend
to the Cherokee, they'll never forget what he did.

(PAUSE)

You get so far in your life, don't you, and you
look back and wonder what it's all been about,
what you've achieved.

I haven't even earned good money.  And I mean,
what else are you for as a bloke? (PAUSE)  My
mother never had to go out to work.

But I'm coming to terms with things a bit now.
Since I've been on my own,  had time to think
about it.

## SCENE 30.

MONTE CARLO

F/X: SEAGULLS. A PAVEMENT CAFÉ
WITH PIANO MUSIC COMING FAINTLY
FROM THE INTERIOR.

NEARBY ARE GARDENS WITH
FOUNTAINS, A FEW TOURISTS.

MUSIC: OSCAR PETERSON

1. ROY:       This beer's going down a treat  - as long as I
              don't think about what it cost!

2. EILEEN:    I can't believe I'm doing this -sitting outside the
              Café de Paris in Monte Carlo.

3. ROY:       I never thought the Casino would be as grand as
              that, it's like a big fairy tale palace.

4. EILEEN:    Being here makes you realise we haven't got a
              clue what being rich really is.  We'll never come
              anywhere near this sort of money.

5. ROY:       No, but I have been making a bit of progress.  I
              had a good appraisal.

6. EILEEN:    Did you?  I thought you were expecting to get
              the push  - again.

7. ROY:       I was,  but Andrew thinks I'm a good bloke and
              he's told his boss they need me to look after the
              older customers.

1. ROY:        There's quite a bit of trade to be had from what they call the Saga Spenders.

2. EILEEN:     Oh.

3. ROY:        Aren't you going to congratulate me?

4. EILEEN:     Like you congratulated me when I got my promotion?

5. ROY:        (PAUSE) I was having a bad time.

6. EILEEN:     I'd been having a bad time as well, but I got no sympathy.

7. ROY:        No. I didn't want to know, did I?

8. EILEEN:     No, you were thinking only about yourself, just like my Dad always did.

9. ROY:        Your Dad, even when he died he carried on causing trouble between us.

10.EILEEN:     I don't call leaving me money causing trouble.

11.ROY:        Your Dad never liked me, never thought I was good enough. He must have thought he'd really timed it well, going when he did.

12.EILEEN:     That's not funny.

13.ROY:        No. Sorry.

14.EILEEN:     You can't blame my Dad, or Michelle for what happened between us. I wasn't happy, Roy. I hadn't been happy for a long time, and you never even noticed.

1. ROY:        I did.  I asked you what you wanted, and all you said was 'More than this'.

               Have you found it, what you want?

2. EILEEN;     (PAUSE) Shall we move on?

               ## F/X: CHAIRS MOVED

3. ROY:        (PAUSE) O.K.  But, can I take your photo, first - to prove we've been here?

4. EILEEN;     Yes, if you want to.

5. ROY:        Come on, a big smile for me.

               ## F/X: CAMERA CLICKS.

6. ROY:        (MEANING EILEEN)  Lovely. (PAUSE)  Let's make the most of being on our own, shall we? We'll be stuck with Samantha again tomorrow.

7. EILEEN:     Oh, yes. (LAUGHS) I'd rather be stuck with you than with her!

8. ROY:        Oh, I'll take that as a compliment - seeing as I'm desperate.

## SCENE 31.

### F/X:  IN THE BACKGROUND MONACO, SEAGULLS, QUIET STREETS.

1. ROY:   V/O:  It was great to be walking around with Eileen like that again.  I put my arm round her at one point, but she moved away - doesn't want me getting ideas.  (LAUGHS) A bit late to tell me that!

## SCENE 32.

TRAIN INTERIOR.

F/X: FAINT BACKGROUND OF BEING IN
THE COMPARTMENT OF A TRAIN
RUNNING ALONG THE COAST.

1. ROY:     It was a wonderful journey back - sitting
            together on the train.  It goes right along the
            edge of the coast, so there you are looking out at
            sunshine on a blue sea and little corners of
            Paradise.

            I didn't want to get off that train.

                 (PAUSE)

            God, I don't want a divorce.  A divorce to me
            just means two people on their own again.

## SCENE 33.

FX:  NICE.  A SQUARE A LITTLE WAY
FROM THE SEA FRONT.   SEAGULLS,
DISTANT TRAFFIC, SHRILL BRASS BAND
BEGINNING TO PLAY. CARNIVAL CROWD
IN THE DISTANCE

1. SAMANTHA: Could you please hurry?  We're not supposed to get access to the Carnival floats till tonight - this guy's doing me a special favour.

2. EILEEN:  Oh, yes?

3. ROY:  We don't want to miss the start of the Battle of Flowers parade.

4. SAMANTHA; You won't.

5. EILEEN:  The floats are lining up already, over there.  Oh, Roy, look at them  - everything's made out of flowers.  See that girl in the huge crinoline it's all carnations and daisies.

6. SAMANTHA: Yes, that's a good one.  Let's see if we can get a photo of you on it now, then I won't have to bother later.  Come on!

F/X: LAUGHTER AND SHOUTS, MUSIC IN
THE BACKGROUND

7. SAMANTHA: Come on, get up there,  Eileen!

8. ROY:  Hey.  Don't shove her like that!

F/X: CAMERA SHUTTER

1. SAMANTHA: Put your arm up to touch the flowers.   And can we have a smile, please?

F/X: CAMERA SHUTTER

2. ROY:      Here, let me give you a hand down, love, are you all right?

3. EILEEN:   (UPSET) Yes, I'm OK.  Oh, look, I've laddered my tights.

4. SAMANTHA: Right, we do the photo with the Carnival parade stuff now.  Hurry up!  Will you get a move on!

5. ROY:      No.  Not till you apologise to my wife.

6. SAMANTHA: What?

7. EILEEN:   Leave it, Roy, she wouldn't understand if you explained it to her.

8. ROY:      We've had enough, Samantha.

9. SAMANTHA: What do you mean?

10.ROY;      You bossing us around all the time, and making rude comments about Eileen.

11.SAMANTHA: You have to have your photos taken  - it's what the magazine is paying for.

12.ROY:      Yes, I know.  And we'll do these Carnival photos, but that'll be it.  After that you leave us alone. You can just beggar off with that assistant manager you've been chatting up and we'll all be a lot happier.

A SILENCE

1. SAMANTHA: Right.  That's OK by me.  Here are your tickets for the Battle of Flowers.  Your seats are in the stand opposite the Negresco, you know, the large pink and white hotel with the minaret?

2. EILEEN: Yes, we do know.  What about the tickets for the King of the Circus Parade tonight?

3. ROY: And the one tomorrow, the flowers and the Circus combined, isn't it?

4. SAMANTHA: I'll leave all your tickets at the hotel reception for you.  Now can we go and get this over with?

## SCENE 34.

F/X: NICE AND CARNIVAL BANDS ETC

FAINTLY IN THE BACKGROUND

1. EILEEN:   V/O  He never stands up to people.

You can't believe the size of the models on the
floats - the ringmaster is about four storeys
high, and then there's all these big papier
mache heads people wear - lions, crocodiles -
all sorts.

Samantha made Roy stand underneath this
giant clown and wear a hat with bells on, so he
looked a clown too.  He put up with it - like he
does.

Ever since we've been married, it's always been
me who's had to make the complaints and do
the organising.

I suppose I do get a bit bossy sometimes, but he
knows it's just my way of looking after him.
And he likes being looked after.

Samantha got this showgirl in a slinky low cut
dress to drape herself over him for one photo  -
to get back at me I suppose.

## SCENE 35.

A STAND ON THE PROMENADE DES
ANGLAIS

F/X:  THE SEA, SEAGULLS AND THE
SOUNDS FROM THE PARADE - CROWD
LAUGHING AND SHOUTING.VARIOUS
BANDS - MARCHING DRUMMERS  AND
BRASS, LATIN AMERICAN ETC

A MAN WALKS PAST SELLING HATS,
WHISTLES ETC

1. VENDOR: Les chapeaux!  Les ficelles!  Tous les jouets de
Carnaval!

F/X: MUSIC, AND CHEERS FROM THE
CROWD CONTINUE AS FLOATS PASS.

2. EILEEN: Oh, look at this one with the Japanese girl on a
little bridge  - isn't she lovely!

3. ROY: Hey, watch out, here comes that guy on stilts,
the one with all the weird make-up on.

4. EILEEN: Oh, yes!  Oh, he's looking at me!

F/X: LAUGHTER AND CHEERS OF
ENCOURAGEMENT FROM THE CROWD
AROUND THEM

5. ROY: He's coming to give you a kiss.

6. EILEEN: (PLEASED)  Me! Oh.

1. ROY:      No, you're all right, he's going for that woman
             with the blonde hair.

2. EILEEN:   Oh.

3. ROY:      You didn't want him to kiss you, did you?

4. EILEEN:   No.

<u>F/X: FADE OUT CARNIVAL THEN FADE</u>

<u>UP AGAIN IN THE BACKGROUND</u>

5. ROY:      V/O: The last time round they started taking
             the flowers off the floats and throwing them to
             the women in the crowd.

             Eileen kept hoping to catch some, but nobody
             picked her out to throw flowers to. (PAUSE)

             It started to get to her a bit. In the end she was
             running up and down trying to get noticed, and
             I could see she was nearly crying because no-
             one chose her.

             I watched her, and suddenly it was like I hadn't
             really seen her for years.

             I'd just seen this woman being bossy and
             practical, and working hard - and getting older.

             (PAUSE) How can you be married to somebody
             for over twenty five years and not know what
             they really want?

6. EILEEN:   Roy, where are you going?

7. ROY:      I won't be a minute.

## SCENE 36.

### PROMENADE DES ANGLAIS STAND.

### F/X:  FADE UP CARNIVAL AGAIN

1. ROY:      V/O:  I'd remembered seeing a flower stall.  All they had left was roses and mimosa.  I bought the lot.

### F/X:  RUSTLE OF BOUQUET

2. ROY:      (APPROACHING) Eileen!  Eileen, love!

3. EILEEN:   Oh.

### A SILENCE

4. ROY:      Hey, you look lovely behind them flowers.

# SCENE 37.

F/X:  THE HOTEL BAR.  PIPED MUSIC IN
THE BACKGROUND 'I WILL ALWAYS
LOVE YOU' WHITNEY HOUSTON

CHRISTOPHE ARRANGES BOTTLES AND
GLASSES BEHIND THE BAR.

1. CHRISTOPHE:    So, you have had a very nice day,
Monsieur Hudson.

2. ROY:      Yes, Christophe, tres bien!

3. CHRISTOPHE:    Will you go to the last day of Carnaval
tomorrow?

4. ROY:      Yes, we're going to the parade and to the
Carnival concert afterwards.

5. CHRISTOPHE:    Another big day for you and your wife.

6. ROY:      Yeah. (PAUSE) That's why she's gone to bed
early.

7. CHRISTOPHE:    But not you.

8. ROY:      No, not me.   They're hard work. aren't they
women?  It's no good just doing something
right, you've got to say everything just right as
well

9. CHRISTOPHE:    I do not understand.

10.ROY:      No, neither do I. (PAUSE) We've walked miles
today, we got lost on the way back  - ended up
at the Place du Palais.

11.CHRISTOPHE;  Oh, yes.

1. ROY:  There's a memorial on the wall there, to a member of the Resistance, a man called Bobby.

2. CHRISTOPHE:  Oh, yes, Jean Bobichon.

3. ROY:  1944. It's good that people remember. In America they have these black and white metal signs in the street. They have them all over, telling you bits of history - they're a bit short on history in America, so they make the most of any facts they can dig up.

4. CHRISTOPHE  Oh, yes?

5. ROY:  There was one I read - it was about an Indian chief called Tsali. He'd given himself up to be executed to save the rest of his people.

6. CHRISTOPHE:  A brave man.

7. ROY:  Yes.  Can I have another beer?

8. CHRISTOPHE:  Bien sur.

### F/X:  A BOTTLE OPENED.

9. ROY:  They used to play this song a lot on the radio when we were in America.  Have you ever been to America?

10. CHRISTOPHE:  No, but I hope to go to Los Angeles soon. To Hollywood.

11. ROY:  Hollywood?

1. CHRISTOPHE:   Yes. I have written a script, a film, and in May I shall go to the festival of film in Cannes, and I shall sell it.

2. ROY:   Will you?

3. CHRISTOPHE:   I will try. Pourquoi pas? Why not?

4. ROY:   Yes, pourquoi pas? Good for you. See if you can make it, eh?. You'll never know until you try.

5. CHRISTOPHE:   Yes. I have always wanted to do this, and this year I shall do it - if they laugh at me, too bad.

6. ROY:   Good for you. Like you say, why not? You only live once. I used to want to be a singer.

7. CHRISTOPHE:   Oh? And you have tried this?

8. ROY:   No. Not really. Too late now.

9. CHRISTOPHE;   But it is a regret?

10.ROY:   Yes, like a lot of other things, it is a regret.

## SCENE 38.

## F/X: DRUM BEAT

1. ROY:　　V/O　I wish I'd had the courage to have a go like Christophe's doing..

Sometimes you feel like a little man in the background in one of those Lowry paintings  - if you rubbed him out it wouldn't matter if he'd been there or not.

At least Tsali would have known what his life was for in the end, how he fitted into the great scheme of things. (PAUSE)  But like Nick said, we can't all be warrior chief.

Anyway I've come through all that now, and  .. . Well,  I know I'm not going to save the world, but . ..there's still a few more days here, still time, for me and Eileen, I hope.

## SCENE 39.

F/X: CONCERT MARQUEE

FAMILY AUDIENCE.  APPLAUSE.

BOOMING PA SYSTEM

1. COMPERE:   Messieurs Mesdames, je vous presente la Musique de Carnaval!

> F/X: CARNIVAL  BAND PLAYS LATIN
>
> AMERICAN MUSIC.   FADE OUT

2. EILEEN:   It was a wonderful atmosphere at the concert, we were all enjoying ourselves like children. The compere was asking people to go up on stage and sing with him.

   They started playing 'La Vie en Rose'.  And Roy went up.  I tried to stop him, I was frightened they'd laugh at him. But he just looked at me and said quietly, 'If I don't do it now, when am I going to do it?'

> F/X FADE UP PIANO PLAYING 'LA VIE EN
>
> ROSE'.

3. COMPERE:   Ah, un Anglais.  Don't be shy, sir!

> F/X: AUDIENCE LAUGHS

4. COMPERE:   You know this song?

5. ROY:       Yes, but only the English words.

6. COMPERE;   That's O K - en anglais OK?

> F/X: CROWD SHOUTS OK

1. ROY:      (SINGS, SHAKILY AT FIRST)  Take me to your
             heart again,   Let's make a start again  Forgiving
             and forgetting

             <u>(HIS SINGING CONTINUES IN THE</u>

             <u>BACKGROUND DURING EILEEN'S V/O)</u>

2. ROY:      Take me to your heart again, and leave behind
             from then, a life of lone regretting

3. EILEEN:   V/O  It's terrible the way things that you do can
             send your life the wrong way.  (PAUSE) I'd kept
             thinking about the mistakes you can make that
             can ruin your life. And how you have to live with
             them.  And what Nick said - 'Why?'

             <u>PAUSE</u>

             Roy was really brave, getting up on that stage to
             sing - and they didn't laugh, they went quiet
             and listened to him.  They loved him.

             And they were looking at me, because it was
             obvious he was singing it to me.   And I cried.   I
             never cry, me. But seeing him looking at me
             like that.

             <u>(SHE'S OVERCOME FOR A MOMENT)</u>

             Seeing him up there, having the moment he'd
             secretly always dreamed of, -   for the first time
             I really understood, saw what his life had been -
             from his point of view.

             <u>F/X:  PIANO MUSIC CONTINUES</u>

## **SCENE 40.**

HOTEL BEDROOM

F/X: BALCONY WINDOW OPEN.  DISTANT
SOUND OF A FEW CARNIVAL REVELLERS
PASSING ON THE PROMENADE BELOW.
BAND FAINTLY IN THE BACKGROUND

1. ROY:      We'll have a good view of the fireworks from our
             balcony.  Looks like there's quite a big crowd
             coming again, but you don't want to go to the
             bonfire,  do you?

2. EILEEN:   No, I don't want to see any of the Carnival
             destroyed.  I want to remember it as it was.

             F/X: ROY CLOSES THE WINDOW AND
             PICKS UP A BOTTLE OF WINE AND
             GLASSES

3. ROY:      Shall we have another glass of this wine?

4. EILEEN:   You've already had two.

5. ROY:      Yes, I know, it's good, isn't it?

             Do you want some more?

6. EILEEN:   Go on, then.  But go steady.

7. ROY:      (LAUGHS)  Will you give over telling me what to
             do?

8. EILEEN:   Somebody has to.

             F/X:  WINE POURED

1. ROY:      You look good, lying on a satin bedspread with a glass of wine in your hand.

2. EILEEN:   Do I?

PAUSE

3. ROY:      I thought we'd go back to Cannes tomorrow.

4. EILEEN:   Oh, yes, I'd like that.  We saw hardly any of it with Samantha marching us around.

5. ROY:      I wonder where she is tonight.

6. EILEEN:   In bed with that bloke, I should think.

7. ROY:      And laughing about us, I expect.

8. EILEEN:   Oh, yes.  She thinks we're too old for any of that.

9. ROY:      (PAUSE) We're not though, are we?

10.EILEEN:   (PAUSE) I don't know.

11.ROY:      Shall we have a go at finding out?

12.EILEEN;   We don't want to miss the firework display.

13.ROY:      We can watch that, afterwards..

PAUSE

14.EILEEN:   You love me, don't you?

15. ROY:     Yeah.

16. EILEEN:  Oh, go on then.  Come over here.

PAUSE

1. ROY:    No. You come over here.

    F/X: MUSIC: 'IT TAKES TWO BABY'

    SONNY & CHER FADE UP FOR A WHILE

    AND THEN FADE OUT AGAIN.

2.ROY:    V/O: I don't know how I managed to play it so cool. But you don't want women taking you for granted, do you?

    I'm actually hoping for early retirement now, so we can be together more. Eileen's going to ask to work part time.

    Like she says, there's plenty of younger people wanting jobs, and we'll have her Dad's money to play with. She's selling the cottage as soon as we get back.

3. EILEEN: V/O: Roy wants me to try to grow a little palm tree in our front garden when we get back. I think it'll be too cold for it, but we can give it a try. He thinks it might impress the neighbours, daft devil.

    We're planning to go back to America and see the Grand Canyon.

    I'll never get into those jeans.

    CREDITS

    MUSIC: YOU'RE THE ONE (SHANIA

    TWAIN)

# A SECOND SUMMER

by

## Liz Wainwright

Original Production
Directed by Marion Nancarrow
BBC Radio 4 Drama
Broadcast 1992
Running Time: 55m

Cast:

| | |
|---|---|
| Cécile | Gwen Watford |
| Alain | David Calder |
| Sophie | Joanna Myers |
| Augustine | Elizabeth Mansfield |
| Mme. Cochet | Barbara Atkinson |
| Mme. Hubert | Barbara Atkinson |
| M. Cochet | Philip Anthony |
| Husband | Philip Anthony |
| Son (18) | William Wortley |

Getting away from Paris and her much loved but very demanding daughter, Cécile needs to reclaim her life. In Normandy she finds help from an unexpected source.

*'I think 'A Second Summer' would make a wonderful film'*

Marion Nancarrow  BBC Drama Producer

## **PROLOGUE**

FX:   BIRDS SING. LOUD HUM OF BEES.

1. AUGUSTINE: (BREATHLESS) Hush, my loved ones. It's
      only your Augustine, come for a little honey.

FX:   SHE LIFTS THE LID OF THE HIVE.

2. SON:      (DISTANT) Mother! Mother!

3. AUGUSTINE: Is there not a minute they will let me alone?
      They'll not come after me here though, not while
      I'm with my honeybees!

4. SON:      (ANGRY) Mother, you come here!

5. AUGUSTINE: Yes.'You come here, and give your last breath
      for me!' Not long, before I do. I'll always be with
      you, though, my lovelies. Poor creatures,
      working till you die. Like me.

## <u>SCENE 1.</u>

<u>FX: A CAR DRIVEN THROUGH HEAVY RAIN</u>

1. CÉCILE: This is it. Saint Martin. Turn left.

2. SOPHIE: Good God, I hope there's nothing coming the other way!

<u>FX: THE CAR CONTINUES ALONG A NARROW LEAFY LANE</u>

3. CÉCILE: There! L'Auberge du Val Fleuri. (SHE SIGHS HAPPILY)

## SCENE 2.

FX:   THE FOYER OF THE INN. PARQUET
FLOOR. IN THE DISTANCE THE CLANK
OF A MOP AND BUCKET. A BEE TAPS
AGAINST THE WINDOW PANE.

1. SOPHIE:  (WHISPERS) Mother, you can't stay here.

2. CÉCILE:  Why not?

3. SOPHIE:  Look at it! Faded curtains, moth-eaten chairs! Come on, we'll find somewhere else. Or you can come back to Paris with me.

4. CÉCILE:  No! (FALTERS) You know what the doctor said.

FX:   THE BEE TAPS AT THE WINDOW
AGAIN AND THEN FLIES INTO THE
HALLWAY. IT BUZZES ROUND SOPHIE
WHO FLICKS IT AWAY.

5. SOPHIE:  Yes, but . . .Oh!

6. CÉCILE:  It's all right, it's only a bee.

7. SOPHIE:  I don't think the doctor meant a holiday in a place like this!

8. CÉCILE:  Sophie. This is what I need. Normandy. Orchards and earth, and big skies.

FX:   FOOTSTEPS APPROACH DOWN THE
STAIRS.

9. SOPHIE:  (EXASPERATED) But not this place! You only chose it because you liked the name! The blossoming valley! Where?

1. CÉCILE: (ALMOST PLEADING) Sophie. Please.

2. SOPHIE: Mother, this place is a dump!

3. CÉCILE: Ssh!

4. ALAIN: (APPROACHING) Good afternoon, ladies.
(SHAKES HANDS) Alain Mercier, at your service.

5. CÉCILE: How do you do? I'm Cécile Clément, and this is
my daughter, Sophie. She's kindly brought me
here. I don't like driving.

6. ALAIN: I am delighted you have come to my little hotel,
Madame Clément. (PAUSE) Humble though it
may seem! Let me take your bags.

7. SOPHIE: Well, actually, I don't think my mother will be
staying]

8. ALAIN: You'd like to see your room, Madame?

9. CÉCILE: (FIRM) Yes. Thank you.

## <u>SCENE 3.</u>

<u>FX:   SLIGHTLY CREAKY DOOR OPENS.</u>
<u>ALAIN PUTS DOWN THE CASES.</u>

1. ALAIN:    I have just finished decorating.

2. CÉCILE:   It's very pretty.

3. ALAIN:    (PLEASED) Yes! (OPENS THE DOOR TO THE BATHROOM) The bathroom isn't modern, of course.

4. SOPHIE:   No.

   <u>PAUSE.</u>

5. ALAIN:    Well, I'll leave you to have a look round.

6. CÉCILE:   Thank you.

SOPHIE WAITS UNTIL HE CLOSES THE DOOR.

7. SOPHIE:   How much deposit did you pay?

8. CÉCILE:   He didn't ask for a deposit.

9. SOPHIE:   Oh. No problem then!

10. CÉCILE: I've made a reservation - for two weeks. The doctor did say I should stay somewhere quiet.

11. SOPHIE: (SIGHS) All right, if it suits you. But you must give me a ring if you decide you want to come back earlier. Promise!

12. CÉCILE: Yes.

1. SOPHIE: Right. (PAUSE) I'll see you, then. Don't bother to come down. (PAUSE) I'll miss you. (PAUSE) Well, take care.

<u>THEY DO NOT KISS</u>

2. CÉCILE: And you.

FX: <u>THE DOOR CLOSES. CÉCILE SIGHS</u> <u>WITH RELIEF.</u>

3. CÉCILE: Oh. Thank you God!

<u>(SHE WALKS ACROSS TO THE WINDOW)</u>

Oh, there's a balcony!

FX: <u>SHE FLINGS OPEN THE FAULTY</u> <u>CASEMENT WINDOW AND STEPS OUT</u> <u>ON TO THE BALCONY. BEES HUM</u> <u>ROUND HER. SHE LAUGHS AND CRIES</u> <u>WITH RELIEF. BEES/MUSIC.</u>

4. AUGUSTINE: So, she has come to us at last, my lovelies. And she must stay. Stay and look after you.

## SCENE 4.

FX:   EARLY MORNING. BIRDS SING IN
THE GARDEN. CÉCILE WALKS THROUGH
THE WET GRASS TOWARDS THE RIVER.
A FISHING LINE IS WOUND IN QUICKLY.

1. ALAIN:   Damn!

2. CÉCILE:   Oh! I'm sorry. I didn't see you there. Did I scare the fish away?

3. ALAIN:   No. It was not his day to be caught. I hate catching them anyway.

4. CÉCILE:   (LAUGHS) Then why fish?

5. ALAIN:   Because I need some trout for dinner.

6. CÉCILE:   Oh. (PAUSE) I'm sorry I disturbed you. I like to take a walk before breakfast when I'm on holiday.

7. ALAIN:   I only wish I could arrange more suitable Maytime weather for you.

8. CÉCILE:   I don't mind the rain. I have my raincoat, and these boots. I bought them specially for country holidays!

9. ALAIN:   Oh, yes! Very er practical. (LAUGHS) Oh, I am sorry!

10. CÉCILE: It's all right. Laurent used to laugh at them, too. (PAUSE) Laurent was my husband. He died just over a year ago.

1. ALAIN:     Ah.

2. CÉCILE:    He always promised me we'd come back to
              Normandy, (PAUSE) but we never did.

3. ALAIN:     So now you have come - here, to my little
              auberge which still needs a lot of renovation,
              and where they give you no breakfast!

4. CÉCILE:    Oh. It's all right. I can wait.

5. ALAIN:     You will have to! (STANDS) Until I get back from
              the village. Here, will you fish while you wait?

6. CÉCILE:    (HESITATES) No, thank you! (LAUGHS)

7. ALAIN:     Then come with me and I will show you the
              village.

8. CÉCILE:    Thank you. Is it far?

9. ALAIN:     No, we can take a short cut across the fields - as
              you have your boots!

              <u>THEY LAUGH.</u>

## SCENE 5.

FX:   ALAIN AND CÉCILE WALK ACROSS
THE FIELDS IN THE BACKGROUND WE
HEAR BEES/MUSIC.

1. CÉCILE:   Have you always lived here?

2. ALAIN:   No. I moved here from Rouen, when my wife
died. I saw the inn and bought it on impulse. I'd
only intended to buy a cottage, that one over
there, with the cherry trees behind it, but . . .

3. CÉCILE:   Oh, beyond the ruined farmhouse?

4. ALAIN:   Yes. That used to be one of the biggest farms
round here, apparently. But after the war
nobody wanted it.

5. CÉCILE:   The cottage looks as if it's still empty. Has no
one bought it?

6. ALAIN:   It's been sold a couple of times - you know,
Parisians or English people looking for a holiday
home. But nobody has stayed for long. They've
not felt welcome.

FX:   BEES/MUSIC INTENSIFIES

7. AUGUSTINE: (LAUGHS) No more they were! Men, all who
came. No good to us. We know what men do,
don't we, my little ones? Set fire to your home
while you're still in there!

(PAUSE)

1. AUGUSTINE: So, she's seen where it lies. Won't be long before she comes to us now.

2. ALAIN: What's the matter?

3. CÉCILE; Nothing. I was just looking at the cottage. Are those bees?

4. ALAIN: Yes. Quite a cluster of them. Bit early for swarming.

5. CÉCILE: They seem to be flying round the roof in a figure eight. Do you see?

6. ALAIN: Yes. I've been told that's how they communicate. They dance in a figure eight to show each other where to go for nectar - none up there, though! Oh, careful, the mud is very slippy here. Take my hand.

7. CÉCILE: (HESITANT) Oh. Thank you.

8. ALAIN: (LAUGHS) It's all right! Are you a timid little soul?

9. CÉCILE: No, not really. I'm just, a little unsure of myself at the moment, but I'll get better. That's what I'm here for.

10. ALAIN: To recover from your bereavement?

11. CÉCILE: In a way.

THEY CONTINUE WALKING.

1. CÉCILE: Oh, is that Saint Martin?

2. ALAIN: Yes, what's left of it. It was a large village once, but now everyone's children want to work in Rouen or Paris.

3. CÉCILE: Like Sophie. She can't understand why I like to be in the country.

4. ALAIN: Is she married?

5. CÉCILE: Separated, unfortunately. But he still writes to her, and to me. Have you any children?

6. ALAIN: Yes, two sons - both married and gone off to make money. And I have a grand-daughter!

7. CÉCILE: Oh, I envy you!

8. ALAIN: Now, welcome to Saint Martin - its bakery, its post office and its cafe - all desperate for gossip. They'll be so glad to see you!

# SCENE 6.

## THE FOYER OF THE HOTEL.

1. SOPHIE: (ON THE TELEPHONE) Mother, where the hell have you hidden my red suit?

2. CÉCILE: Oh, I'm sorry. I took it to be cleaned. The ticket's on the kitchen notice board. I thought I told you.

3. SOPHIE: Oh. Oh, right. I'll pick it up tomorrow, then. I want to wear it for this meeting with Allied Airways. Looks like they're interested in our Customer Services Package.

4. CÉCILE: Oh, very good.

5. SOPHIE: How are you surviving?

6. CÉCILE: I'm fine. I've slept a lot, and read a couple of novels.

7. SOPHIE: I don't suppose you can do much else. I've been watching the weather, you've had nothing but rain!

8. CÉCILE: It hasn't been too bad, and the lounge here is very comfortable.

9. SOPHIE: What are the other guests like?

10. CÉCILE: (HESITANT) There aren't any other guests at the moment. The hotel has only been open a year. But M. Mercier has more bookings for later on in the season.

11. SOPHIE: You're there on your own?

1. CÉCILE; Yes, but M. Mercier has started joining me for dinner, so I'm not lonely.

2. SOPHIE: He's hardly your type, I would have thought. All hairy forearms and baggy trousers!

3. CÉCILE: Sophie!

4. SOPHIE: Look, I can manage to come and fetch you home this weekend if you've had enough.

5. CÉCILE: No! . . . thank you.

6. SOPHIE: It's terribly quiet here on my own.

7. CÉCILE: I must go, I can hear Alain serving dinner.

8. SOPHIE: Alain?

9. CÉCILE: M. Mercier. Now don't worry about me, I'm fine. Goodbye!

# SCENE 7.

FX:   THE DINING ROOM. ALAIN AND
CÉCILE ARE FINISHING THEIR EVENING
MEAL.

1. ALAIN:    So you hope Sophie and her husband will get back together again?

2. CÉCILE:   Yes. Philippe's a lovely man, but they married too soon after my husband's death. Sophie wanted him to take Laurent's place and indulge her like he did. But Philippe's from the real world where you can't just have everything.

3. ALAIN:    But he still wants her?

4. CÉCILE:   Oh, yes. He's waiting for her to grow up, he says.

5. ALAIN:    And will she?

6. CÉCILE:   I don't know. We weren't very sensible parents, Laurent and I. We gave her too much. But I needed someone to love me, and Laurent was so delighted to have a daughter at last. He was older than me. There were no children from his first marriage.

7. ALAIN:    And you had not been married before?

8. SOPHIE:   No. (PAUSE) Sophie was devastated when Philippe left her. She couldn't cope with losing him as well as her father.

9. ALAIN:    So you let her move back in with you?

10. CÉCILE: What else could I do? I'm her mother.

1. ALAIN:    And now?

2. CÉCILE:    What do you mean?

3. ALAIN:    You want to get away from her.

4. CÉCILE:    No, of course not!

5. ALAIN:    I think you do.

6. CÉCILE:    No! I just came here for a rest. The doctor said I needed a break.

PAUSE

7. ALAIN:    Would you like some more coffee?

8. CÉCILE:    No, thank you. (FORMAL) But thank you for a lovely meal.

ALAIN LAUGHS LOUDLY.

9. CÉCILE:    Why are you laughing at me?

10. ALAIN:    I'm sorry. It's just, you are so polite. Like a child who's been asked to tea in some grand house. Are you always so careful to please people?

11. CÉCILE: (SNAPS) Yes! I am! I've had to be - all my damned life! (ALMOST IN TEARS) Excuse me!

SHE GETS UP CLUMSILY AND HURRIES

OUT OF THE DINING ROOM.

## SCENE 8.

FX:   THE LANE. BIRDS. MONSIEUR
COCHET DIGGING WET EARTH AND
RUBBLE. MUSIC/BEES FAINTLY IN THE
BACKGROUND.

1. M. COCHET: Afternoon, Madame.

2. CÉCILE:   Good afternoon, Monsieur Cochet. That looks
like heavy work.

3. M. COCHET: Yes. The rain has washed down all this
rubble and blocked the drain.

4. CÉCILE:   Oh dear. (PAUSE) I was wondering if I might
have a look round the cottage. Les Cerisiers. M.
Mercier said you were the one to ask?

5. M. COCHET: That's right. I'm keeping an eye on it for an
agent in Rouen. I'll show you round!

## **SCENE 9.**

FX. THE COTTAGE. STONE FLOOR.
RATTLING WINDOW. DOOR OFF ITS
HINGES. MUSIC/BEES.

1. AUGUSTINE: I told you! Didn't I promise you she would come!

2. M. COCHET: (LIFTING OPEN THE DOOR) Good solid door if it was fixed.

FX:   THEY ENTER THE COTTAGE. THE
MUSIC/BEES INTENSIFIES.

3. CÉCILE:   (SIGHS) Oh.

4. M. COCHET: Not a big place. Monsieur Grevet built the other house for his second wife. She wasn't one to slave in the kitchen all day like the first poor creature - well, that's what my mother tells me.

5. CÉCILE:   Your mother knows the owners?

6. M. COCHET: Used to. She's ninety two now, but when she was a girl she used to work for the Grevets. You can go and visit them if you like - they're all in the churchyard!

7. AUGUSTINE: (WHISPERS) Yes. But not me. You'll not find me there. I stayed here with you, didn't I, my lovelies? Like I promised.

8. CÉCILE:   (WALKING THROUGH) And this was the kitchen?

9. M. COCHET: Yes. (SHIVERS) Always cold in here, even with the sun shining in.

1. CÉCILE:   What a lovely view out into the garden. And look at all the bees round that clematis!

2. M. COCHET: Yes. If you want to have a good look round, you can do. I've got to go and finish clearing that muck.

3. CÉCILE:   Oh. Yes. I would like to stay for a while. Is it all right if I walk up as far as the orchard?

4. M. COCHET: Walk as far as you like!

## SCENE 10.

FX: MUSIC/BEES. CÉCILE CLIMBS THE
OLD WOODEN STAIRCASE TO THE
LANDING AND BEDROOMS. SHE TALKS
TO HERSELF.

1. CÉCILE: Two bedrooms. (SHE WALKS ACROSS THE
ROOM) Oh, this one looks out on the orchard.

FX: A BEE BUZZES AGAINST THE
WINDOW PANE. CÉCILE OPENS THE
WINDOW. DISTANT TRACTOR.
BIRDSONG, MORE BEES APPROACH.

2. AUGUSTINE: Yes, come near and take a look at her, my
lovelies. She will stay. She must stay and take
care of you, so that I may go to my rest, at last.

3. CÉCILE: Wonderful!

FX: SHE SIGHS AS SHE STAYS A
MOMENT TO ENJOY THE VIEW. THEN
SHE CLOSES THE WINDOW AND GOES
BACK DOWN THE STAIRS. SHE WALKS
INTO THE KITCHEN AGAIN, TURNS ON
THE TAP.

4. CÉCILE: Running water anyway, (SHE FLICKS A
SWITCH) and electricity. I know what Laurent
would have said. 'Think about it, Cécile. Cold
and wet in the winter. Miles from a town. And
what about Sophie?' (PAUSE) (ANGRILY) And
what about me?

FX:   SHE DRAGS OPEN THE KITCHEN
DOOR AND GOES OUT INTO THE
GARDEN. WE HEAR BIRDS FLY OFF.
THEN SILENCE. THEN BEES ARRIVE.

## SCENE 11.

FX:   THE DINING ROOM. ALAIN SERVES
THE VEGETABLES.

1. ALAIN:   More potatoes?

2. CÉCILE:   Yes, please!

3. ALAIN:   Ah! - a real appetite at last! (PAUSE) You seem happier this evening.

4. CÉCILE:   Yes. I'm sorry I was so silly last night.

5. ALAIN:   It was good to know you can be angry.

6. CÉCILE:   I never realised how angry till these last few months.

7. ALAIN:   Tell me. No. Eat first, have a few glasses of wine, and then we can talk. As friends.

8. CÉCILE:   Yes.

## SCENE 12.

FX:   THE LOUNGE. WIND AND RAIN
OUTSIDE.

CÉCILE AND ALAIN ENTER.

1. ALAIN:     I'll put some more logs on the fire. Would you draw the curtains, shut out the wind and rain.

FX:   THE FIRE CRACKLES AS IT SEIZES THE LOGS. WE HEAR THE CURTAINS CLOSE.

2. CÉCILE:    The weather forecast promised a bit more sunshine tomorrow.

3. ALAIN:     Yes, at last! Now, I recommend a large cognac and this ancient but comfortable armchair by the fire.

4. CÉCILE:    (SIGHS) Would you mind if I took off my shoes and curled up?

5. ALAIN:     I would be delighted to see you so 'at home'. (PAUSE) What's wrong?

6. CÉCILE:    Oh, just that word 'home'. A very elusive concept.

7. ALAIN:     Is it?

8. CÉCILE:    The last time I went somewhere I called 'home' was when my parents died. Laurent and I had a flat in Paris and a house near Geneva, but I never thought of them as 'home'.

PAUSE.

1. CÉCILE:  My parents thought living in Paris meant you were a success. That's why I went to work there. I knew they would be thrilled to talk about it to their friends. And I thought it would be exciting of course. In those days I was a great one for so called 'excitement'.

2. ALAIN:  Nothing wrong with that.

3. CÉCILE:  Excitement kills people!

PAUSE.

4. ALAIN:  Oh, I see. Who?

5. CÉCILE:  The only man I ever loved.

6. ALAIN:  Laurent?

7. CÉCILE:  No. I loved Laurent, but the second love isn't the same. No. His name was David. I met him when I was twenty. I was a different person then. Confident, ambitious - and reckless. (LAUGHS) Can you believe that?

8. ALAIN:  (DRYLY) No.

9. CÉCILE:  He was wonderful, but that wasn't enough for me - I wanted him to be as daredevil as I was. I made him go skiing, on a dangerous piste, early one morning while the snow was still soft. There had been a warning of avalanche, but I wouldn't listen.

PAUSE

1. ALAIN: And you will never forget.

2. CÉCILE: No. (PAUSE) I died with him in a way. Oh, I carried on with my so called career, my life - but ever since then, it's been as if the person living that life were someone else.

3. ALAIN: Even when you married Laurent?

4. CÉCILE: Especially when I married Laurent. I feel I've been pretending, playing a part all my life.

5. ALAIN: We all do - at least some of the time.

6. CÉCILE: But I want to stop. I want to live in reality again. Does that sound stupid?

7. ALAIN: No. (HE POKES AT THE FIRE) But you have to find your reality. We each have our own which we choose to live in. Mine is here - playing the part of 'le patron' in a small country hotel.

8. CÉCILE: And you're happy.

9. ALAIN: Yes. Lonely sometimes, but content. (PAUSE) Were you not happy with Laurent?

10. CÉCILE: Sometimes. It gave me some confidence again, just being with him. And I learned to accept that he wanted other women as well as me. I wasn't going to try to change someone again.

PAUSE.

He was one of those strong-willed people who had a sort of charm, a facility for making everyone do what he wanted. Sophie is the same.

1. ALAIN: And what she wants is you to live with her in Paris.

2. CÉCILE: Yes. (PAUSE) When Laurent died - it's terrible to say this - but I felt as if he'd set me free. With the money he left, I no longer needed to feel grateful to anyone. All my life I'd felt I'd had to be grateful - to him, to my hard working parents. Now I could be free . . .

3. ALAIN: If Sophie would let you.

4. CÉCILE: Yes.

5. ALAIN: And will you go back to Paris, just because she wants you to?

6. CÉCILE: (SIGHS) Yes.

7. ALAIN: She made you ill with her demands and her selfish possessiveness! And you'll still go back and live with her?.

8. CÉCILE: She needs me. I'll have to go back. (PAUSE) But not yet.

9. ALAIN: You are going to stay here a little longer.

10. CÉCILE: Yes.

# SCENE 13.

1. SOPHIE:  (ON THE TELEPHONE) What do you mean, no?

2. CÉCILE:  I'd like to stay for another week or two.

3. SOPHIE:  You can't. I have to fly to New York on Sunday. This Allied Airways deal is turning into a big contract. They want to commission us to design another system for them. I'll be there at least three weeks.

4. CÉCILE:  Well, that's all right then.

5. SOPHIE:  How are you going to get home, if I'm not there to fetch you?

6. CÉCILE:  I can stay here as long as Iike - I've asked Alain.

7. SOPHIE:  Oh, have you! But what about the flat? It will be left empty.

8. CÉCILE:  The concierge will keep an eye on things.

9. SOPHIE:  But I thought you would be there. I told Rachel she could stay with us while she's over for the Marketing Conference.

10. CÉCILE:  Can't she book into a hotel?

11. SOPHIE:  (SURPRISED) Mother?

12. CÉCILE:  I'm sorry, I have to go now, Sophie. Have a good trip. Goodbye!

> HESITANTLY CÉCILE PUTS DOWN THE
> RECEIVER, HEARING SOPHIE STILL
> SHOUTING 'MOTHER' DOWN THE
> PHONE. SLOWLY CÉCILE EXHALES.

## SCENE 14.

<u>THE VILLAGE STREET. A DOG BARKING.
THE WHIRR OF A MOTO-CYCLETTE. THE
SHOP BELL PINGS AS CÉCILE LEAVES
THE BOULANGERIE.</u>

1. MME HUBERT:   Goodbye, Madame Clément. Bon appetit!

2. CÉCILE:   Thank you. (ALMOST COLLIDES WITH COCHET) Oh, M. Cochet, I was going to come and see you.

3. M. COCHET: Hello, Madame. Treating yourself to Mme Hubert's pastries?

4. CÉCILE:   Yes, I like to take a picnic on my afternoon walk. Can I ask you about the cottage?

5. M. COCHET: Of course.

6. CÉCILE:   You said that it was for sale. Do you think the agent would consider allowing someone to rent it?

7. M. COCHET: How long for?

8. CÉCILE:   I don't know. For a month at least.

9. M. COCHET: I would think they'd agree to that. The owner is a man who has a couple of butchers shops in Rouen. He bought it for holidays and weekends - it was him who put in the electrics and that.

10. CÉCILE: Yes, that's a big advantage.

11. M. COCHET:   Wasn't for him, he hated the place in the end! And the people he let it to never stayed long either.

1. CÉCILE:    Well, I'd like to move in as soon as possible. Will you ask the agent for me?

2. M. COCHET: Yes, I'll give him a ring.

3. CÉCILE:    Thank you.

4. M. COCHET: Enjoy your picnic! Where are you walking to this afternoon?

5. CÉCILE:    The churchyard first, then across the fields to the orchard behind the cottage. The cherry trees are in blossom.

6. M. COCHET: The churchyard, eh? Not much chance of conversation there.

7. CÉCILE:    (LAUGHS) No, M. Cochet! At least, I hope not!

## SCENE 15.

FX:   THE CHURCHYARD. CÉCILE WALKS
ALONG THE GRAVEL PATH.
BEES/MUSIC.

1. AUGUSTINE: No. Keep away from them! You go to my orchard. The churchyard's not your place!

FX:   CÉCILE WALKS MORE SLOWLY
ALONG THE PATH AND THEN STOPS.
SHE STEPS THROUGH LONG GRASS.

2. AUGUSTINE:   No! You don't want to go near them! Husbands and children, they're cruel! Give you no peace, no rest!

FX:   CÉCILE PUSHES THE GRASS AWAY
FROM THE GRAVESTONES.

3. CÉCILE:   Georges Grevet, 1862 - 1924. And his sons Albert, Matthieu, and Vincent. With their Father in Heaven.

FX:   A SOFT FOOTSTEP BEHIND HER.

4. M. COCHET: You found them then.

5. CÉCILE:   Oh! Oh, M. Cochet! You frightened me!

6. M. COCHET: (INNOCENT) Did I? I just come to tell you I phoned the agent. They're going to check up how much to charge, but they have no objection to a short term lease. Never thought they'd be so lucky, I reckon. They're going to ring me back tomorrow.

1. CÉCILE:   Oh, thank you.

2. M. COCHET: Well, somebody ought to be living there. Don't like to see a house going to waste. It sheltered these fellas long enough.

3. CÉCILE:   Yes. There's no mention of their mother on the gravestone. Isn't she buried here?

4. M. COCHET: No. She's well away from them. My mother says she screamed at them when she was dying, that if they didn't bury her in the orchard, to be with her honeybees, she'd curse them on their way to hell. The only time she got her own way, according to Mother.

5. CÉCILE:   Oh, how terrible. (PAUSE) Could I come and visit your mother one afternoon? I'd like to know more about the cottage.

6. M. COCHET: Yes, any time, she'll be in. Like she says, she's not going anywhere, God willing!

## SCENE 16.

> FX:   THE ORCHARD. BIRDS SINGING.
> COWS IN THE DISTANCE. CÉCILE WALKS
> THROUGH THE LONG GRASS AND THEN
> SITS DOWN.

1. CÉCILE:   Well, Madame Grevet, I can't find your headstone, so if I'm sitting on your grave I apologise. (SHE UNWRAPS HER CAKE) I love your orchard. I wonder if you ever had time to sit here in the sunshine and eat apricot tart.

> FX:   THE BEES ARRIVE AGAIN, ONE,
> THEN TWO, THEN SEVERAL. CÉCILE
> FINISHES THE CAKE AND SCREWS UP
> THE WRAPPING.

2. CÉCILE:   Oh, I could sleep! (YAWNS) Well, why not?

> FX:   BEES HOVER.

3. AUGUSTINE: Are you watching over her then - like you watch over me? Eight stones mark my grave, but the grass has buried them. Not one of them cared enough to tend my resting place and remember.

> (FX:   THE BEES SOUND LOUDER AND
> MORE FEROCIOUS AS HER ANGER
> MOUNTS)

Curse them! Curse my cruel husband! Curse my unloving sons!

ALAIN APPROACHES.

1. ALAIN:    SLAPS HIS HAT AT THE BEES) Go on! Get away from here!

    FX:   THE SOUND OF THE BEES

    INTENSIFIES UNTIL IT WAKES CÉCILE.

2. CÉCILE:    (WAKING) Oh. Alain.

3. ALAIN:    (WAFTING THE BEES AWAY WITH HIS HAT) Get away!

    FX:   THE BEES RETREAT ANGRILY,

    HOVERING A LITTLE WAY OFF.

4. ALAIN:    I'm sorry, I didn't mean to wake you. But there were bees right above your head. I thought you might get stung.

5. CÉCILE:    I was dreaming, about walking across stepping stones. Eight. I counted them.

6. ALAIN:    (HESITANT) You looked lovely lying there under the cherry blossom.

7. CÉCILE:    (EMBARRASSED) Oh.

8. ALAIN:    (AWKWARD) I came to ask you if you wouldn't mind eating late tonight. I have to go into Rouen for some parts for the boiler.

9. CÉCILE:    Yes, that's fine.

10. ALAIN:    And I've got to get some more groceries, ready for the people arriving next week. If you like, you could come with me.

11. CÉCILE: Yes, that sounds a lovely idea. I'm going to need to do some shopping. I've decided to stay here for the summer. I'm going to rent the cottage.

1. ALAIN:    This place?

2. CÉCILE:    Yes. What's wrong?

3. ALAIN:    (PAUSE) I'm not sure. Just village superstition, I suppose.

4. CÉCILE:    Oh.

5. ALAIN:    You know you're welcome to stay with me as long as you want.

6. CÉCILE:    Yes, but I need a place of my own. I'm still looking for that 'elusive home', and I feel this may be it.

7. ALAIN:    Good. (PAUSE) You know I want you to stay.

8. CÉCILE:    Yes. I know.

# SCENE 17.

## FX:   MADAME COCHET'S SMALL LIVING ROOM. TICKING OF A LARGE CLOCK.

1. MME COCHET:   Augustine her name was. God rest her. They killed her you know.

2. CÉCILE:   Who?

3. MME COCHET:   Her husband, and her sons. Oh, she was poorly - never could breathe right. But the truth is, she died of slavery. Looking after them, and doing farm work. They knew she wasn't strong, but they wouldn't let her have any help till she got bad - then they took me on.

4. CÉCILE:   When did she die?

5. MME COCHET:   1912, just before her fortieth birthday. She should never have married him. He was a good ten year older than her, but she wasn't pretty, so I expect she didn't have much choice. Mind you, what choices do women have, eh?

6. CÉCILE:   Oh, a lot more these days.

7. MME COCHET:   Oh, yes? Still end up somebody's wife, most of them. Still get kids to look after. Suck you dry if you let them!

8. CÉCILE:   (PAUSE) Yes.

9. MME COCHET:   She kept bees - her only friends, she said. She had at least half a dozen bee hives in that orchard. She used to give me honey, oh, it was special! Most of the bees went after she died though.

1. CÉCILE: They're back now. There are dozens of them in the orchard, and in the garden.

2. MME COCHET: Are there? I'd never expected that. Not after what he did to them. The most frightening thing I ever saw.

3. CÉCILE: What?

4. MME COCHET: They kept swarming after she died - looking for her. Nobody told them she was dead, you see. You're supposed to tell the bees, when anything happens to their keeper. I was going to, but I was too scared.

5. CÉCILE: Well, you were only a child.

6. MME COCHET: Yes. So, anyway, he got fed up with them, him and the lads. And frightened too, I reckon. So they set fire to the hives. Terrible flames, and bees like black smoke.

   Mind you, the Grevets suffered for it, stung to death nearly. But that was it, they was gone, and I've never seen many bees there since. How'd you like to make us some coffee to go with these cakes you brought?

   FX:   PAUSE. THE KETTLE BOILS.

   COFFEE IS MADE.

1. CÉCILE:  (STIRRING HER COFFEE) What was she like, Augustine?

2. MME COCHET:  Not tall, but not as little as you, and very thin. (DRINKS NOISILY) She had long brown hair tied back. Oh, and she was kind! Always wanting to please people, always grateful for anything you did for her. (EATS CAKE, LICKS HER FINGERS) She wanted loving, but they didn't love her - not even her sons. Followed their father too much. She worked herself into her grave to give them what they wanted. Children don't realise, do they?

3. CÉCILE:  (PAUSE) No.

4. MME COCHET:  And it was all for nothing. 1914 saw to that. (PAUSE) So, you're liking it at the cottage then?

5. CÉCILE:  Yes. There was a lot to do to make it habitable, of course, but Alain, M. Mercier has helped me.

6. MME COCHET:  Oh, yes?

7. CÉCILE:  Tell me, was it once one of a row of cottages?

8. MME COCHET:  No. Never.

9. CÉCILE:  But there's a number eight carved by the door.

10. MME COCHET: Oh, that was her. She couldn't write, so that was how she signed her name. A figure eight, for the eighth month - Augustine.

## **SCENE 18.**

FX:   THE COTTAGE GARDEN. CÉCILE IS DIGGING AND PLANTING SEEDLINGS.

BEES/MUSIC IN THE BACKGROUND.

1. AUGUSTINE: There, you see, my lovelies, she's planting flowers for you - like they should have planted on my grave. She will take care of you. I have whispered to her that she must stay.

2. ALAIN:   (APPROACHING) You should be wearing a hat.

3. CÉCILE:   Oh, Alain! No, I shouldn't - I'm enjoying the sunshine.

4. ALAIN:   What are you planting?

5, CÉCILE:   Pansies, and petunias. And geraniums in those pots. (STANDS, EASING HER BACK) My back will never be the same again, but they'll look so beautiful when they're in full flower.

6. ALAIN:   I only hope you'll be here to see them. Sophie has phoned. Just got back from New York.

7. CÉCILE:   Oh.

8. ALAIN:   She couldn't believe you'd rented the cottage. She's coming the day after tomorrow. To help you pack your bags, I think.

9. CÉCILE:   Oh. Oh, dear.

10. ALAIN:   You're not going back with her, are you?

1. CÉCILE: I hope not. But how do I say no? I've never been any good at saying no to Sophie.

FX:   BEES ARE HEARD

2. ALAIN: She doesn't need you.

3. CÉCILE: Yes, she does. We all need someone to put an arm round us.

4. ALAIN: Yes.

FX:   PAUSE. WE HEAR THE BEES GATHERING, AND ECHOES FROM AUGUSTINE'S PAST - SON CALLING.

5. AUGUSTINE: (WHISPERS) Oh, let me be! You torment me!

6. CÉCILE: Sophie's very persuasive, you know. Like her father. And she's vulnerable. She's always been used to being looked after.

7. SON: Mother! Mother!

8. AUGUSTINE: No, I'm tired!

9. ALAIN: You don't want to go back to Paris.

10. CÉCILE: (WHISPERS) She's here - again.

11. ALAIN: Cécile?

12. CÉCILE: (DISTRACTED) What? No, but I may have to, for a while at least. Till Sophie gets used to the idea.

13. ALAIN: If you go now, she'll never let you come back.

FX:   THE SOUND OF THE BEES INTENSIFIES ANGRILY AND COMES CLOSER.

1. CÉCILE:   Alain, she's my daughter. You can't deny your children.

2. AUGUSTINE: They expect too much. Always wanting! Always wanting me!

3. SON:   Mother! You come here, damn you!

4. HUSBAND:   Augustine! Call yourself a wife! Come here!

5. AUGUSTINE: (IN TEARS) No! No! Oh, I wish I wasn't a mother! And I should never have been a wife!

6. ALAIN:   Cécile! What is it?

7. CÉCILE; I don't know! Alain, I think I'm going mad. I keep hearing voices! In the kitchen, and out here in the garden.

8. ALAIN:   Oh. You're not the first. Perhaps you shouldn't have moved in here.

9. CÉCILE:   No, it's right that I'm here. I feel somehow, protected. She wants me here.

10. ALAIN:   She?

FX:   THE BEES COME CLOSER

11. CÉCILE: But what can I do? Sophie will be determined to take me back to Paris, and I don't think I've the strength to go against her.

1. AUGUSTINE: No! You must stay. They need you! You must stay! Stay!

2. CÉCILE: (AFRAID) Oh!

FX: THE SOUND OF THE BEES GROWS LOUDER

3. ALAIN: Oh, in the name of God! Look at that! The bees are swarming! Come on! We'd better get inside!

FX: HE PULLS CÉCILE TOWARDS THE COTTAGE. THE BEES SWARM TOWARDS THEM.

CÉCILE CRIES OUT. ALAIN THRUSTS OPEN THE DOOR OF THE COTTAGE.

4. ALAIN: Quick! (HE SLAMS THE DOOR) Cécile! Cécile!

FX; THE BUZZING REACHES A CRESCENDO, AS IF PUSHING AGAINST THE DOOR.

5. CÉCILE: (ALMOST FAINTING) She's here. Oh, Alain!

6. ALAIN: It's all right! Let me hold you. It's all right.

THE NOISE SUBSIDES A LITTLE.

7. ALAIN: (A LITTLE FRIGHTENED) Oh, they're moving away. Can you see them? Over your plants. Hundreds of them. Like a tower, no, like a figure eight!

8. CÉCILE: (WHISPERS) Augustine!

## **SCENE 19.**

### FX:   THE KITCHEN. CÉCILE IS CHOPPING TOMATOES ETC. FOR A SALAD.

1. CÉCILE:   Would you mix the dressing, Sophie? There's oil and vinegar in the corner cupboard.

2. SOPHIE:   O.K. It's like being back at home, isn't it? Preparing for a dinner party.

3. CÉCILE:   (LAUGHS NERVOUSLY) I don't think Alain coming for supper will be quite the same sort of occasion. He's quite happy with cheese, a bowl of salad, and a bottle of red wine on the kitchen table.

4. SOPHIE:   You seem to have become quite close friends.

5. CÉCILE:   Yes.

6. SOPHIE:   Is that why you wanted to stay here? Because of him?

7. CÉCILE:   No. Because of me.

8. SOPHIE:   Oh. (PAUSE) But you do understand why I want you to come back to Paris with me tomorrow?

9. CÉCILE:   Yes, I understand.

10. SOPHIE: You've had a good long holiday.

11. CÉCILE: Yes.

1. SOPHIE: Look, if you really want to, we can stay till the end of the week. I'll phone the office in the morning.

2. CÉCILE: Thank you. I would like to stay. In fact I think I'd like to live here.

3. SOPHIE: (DELIBERATELY MISUNDERSTANDING) Yes, I know you like being in the country. But you'll love getting back to Paris. Haven't you missed the shops, and the concerts?

4. CÉCILE: No. I told you, I'm happy here. Happier than I've been for years!

5. SOPHIE: Mother. It's horrible being in the flat without you. It's just like when Philippe went. (PAUSE) I don't think I'll ever get over that, you know.

6. CÉCILE: You could ask him to come back.

7. SOPHIE: No! Oh, no. You don't know what I went through! How would you have felt if Daddy had walked out on you! You couldn't have coped!

8. CÉCILE: (PAUSE) Couldn't I?

PAUSE

9. SOPHIE: Daddy wouldn't have thought much of this place!

10. CÉCILE: No. We did stay in Normandy once, though, when we were first married. But we never came back.

1. SOPHIE: I only remember seaside holidays. Nice and Sardinia. Didn't Daddy look good on a beach - all the women used to catch their breath when he walked past, didn't they?

2. CÉCILE: (RUEFUL) Oh, yes.

3. SOPHIE: Those were wonderful holidays!

4. CÉCILE: For you and Laurent, yes. (PAUSE) But I remember that after our holidays in Cannes or Biarritz, or wherever, I used to wish I could have a second holiday. Away from the heat and the crowds. A second summer, somewhere cool and green and quiet. (PAUSE) I want that now, Sophie. I want to stay here. To live here.

5. SOPHIE: I know, and it would be lovely, but it's just not practicable!

6. CÉCILE: You sound just like your father!

7. SOPHIE: What's wrong with that?

8. CÉCILE: (PAUSE) Nothing. (TRYING NOT TO CRY) Oh, I'm sorry.

9. SOPHIE: Oh, for heaven's sake! What is the matter with you? I thought the doctor sent you on holiday to get better, not to get even more nervous and uptight!

10. CÉCILE: Sophie, I don't wish to come back and live with you! It's not what I want to do with my life! (FALTERING) And it, it's not good for me!

1. SOPHIE:  Oh. (PAUSE) Is it the cooking, and everything at the flat? Is it getting too much for you?

2. CÉCILE:  No.

3. SOPHIE:  I thought it was helping you to get over Daddy. Being with me, and entertaining my friends like you used to entertain his. You always liked looking after people.

4. CÉCILE:  I liked to please your father.

5. SOPHIE:  (PATRONISING) And you did.

6. CÉCILE:  (ANGRY) Not enough, or he wouldn't have . . .

7. SOPHIE:  What?

8. CÉCILE:  Made love to other women!

PAUSE

9. SOPHIE:  (COLDLY) He didn't. Daddy wasn't like that! You're mad!

PAUSE

10. CÉCILE: (IN TEARS, WONDERING) Am I? Am I?

## SCENE 20.

THE LIVING ROOM OF THE
COTTAGE. ALAIN PUSHES BACK HIS
CHAIR, READY TO LEAVE.

1. CÉCILE: Are you sure you won't stay for coffee, Alain?

2. ALAIN: No. Thank you.

3. SOPHIE: It's been very nice to meet you, Monsieur Mercier.

PAUSE.

4. ALAIN: Yes. Thank you for the meal.

5. CÉCILE: So formal, Alain!

6. ALAIN: Will I see you tomorrow?

7. SOPHIE: I think we'll be packing tomorrow.

8. ALAIN: But I thought you and your mother were going to stay a few more days at least. Aren't you, Cécile?

9. CÉCILE: Well, yes, Sophie - I thought you said . . .

10. SOPHIE: I don't think it's such a good idea to wait after all.

11. CÉCILE: Oh.

12. ALAIN: Here's your cardigan, Cécile. You're going to walk me to the end of the lane, aren't you . . . (LYING) like you usually do.

13. CÉCILE: Oh. Yes. I won't be long, Sophie.

ALAIN CLOSES THE DOOR.

## SCENE 21.

### THEY WALK DOWN THE GARDEN PATH AND INTO THE LANE.

1. ALAIN: (ANGRY) Can't you see what she's doing, Cécile! She's taking over your life again. Look at the way she had you this evening - dressed up as if it was a restaurant, serving the meal when she said so. For goodness sake!

### THEY CONTINUE WALKING.

2. ALAIN: Cécile! Are you listening to me!

3. CÉCILE: Yes. I'm listening.

4. ALAIN: You can't go back to live like that. I won't let you!

5. CÉCILE: You won't let me! Who are you to "let me"? I make my own decisions.

6. ALAIN: Ha! Cécile . . .

7. CÉCILE: Goodnight, Alain.

8. ALAIN: (HURT) I think you mean goodbye.

### ALAIN WALKS ON DOWN THE LANE.CÉCILE STANDS THERE SILENTLY FOR A MOMENT.

9. CÉCILE: (WHISPERS) Goodbye.

### SHE WALKS BACK UP THE LANE.IN THE DISTANCE SOPHIE CALLS FOR HER.

10. SOPHIE: Mother! Mother!

## SCENE 22.

### CÉCILE WALKS INTO THE ORCHARD.

1. CÉCILE: (TO HERSELF) Not yet. Just a few more minutes to say goodbye to the cherry trees. We could always come back next year to see them in blossom.

PAUSE.

That's what Laurent said - that we'd come back.

Alain's right. I'll be going back to Paris and to Sophie's life, her way of doing things. Just like her father - demanding that the table is always perfect - no piece of cheese and bowl of salad on the kitchen table for him! "Standards, " he used to say, " I have standards, Cécile."

(WITH IRONY) Oh, yes!

No. Not those thoughts! I've hurt Sophie enough.

But she doesn't know what it costs, to give everything - to have no time, no space, nothing left for yourself.

Augustine knew what it cost - your life!

# SCENE 23.

## IN THE KITCHEN.

## SOPHIE IS PACKING CROCKERY INTO A BOX.

## CÉCILE ENTERS.

1. SOPHIE: Where have you been! Didn't you hear me calling?

2. CÉCILE: What are you doing?

3. SOPHIE: Packing. You don't intend to leave all these things in the cottage, do you? Of course, we'll have to get rid of most of it when we get back - it won't do for Paris. Honestly, some of these things! Your standards seem to have dropped considerably since you've been here!

   PAUSE.

   You'll soon be back in the swing of things. Dominique and Simone said they'd come for dinner next week. In fact there are several people we ought to invite. Oh, and I got tickets for Faust. I know you don't like opera, but my boss is going and there'll be a little party afterwards.

4. CÉCILE: Have you seen my book?

5. SOPHIE: Oh, it's a bit late to start reading now, isn't it? Come on, bed time.

## <u>SCENE 24.</u>

<u>FX:   THE COTTAGE BEDROOM. CÉCILE</u>

<u>AND SOPHIE ARE GOING TO BED.</u>

1. CÉCILE:   I'm sorry we're having to share, but the other bedroom is still full of old furniture and rubbish.

2. SOPHIE:   (TRYING TO CLOSE THE SASH WINDOW) It's all right. This window needs fixing. I can't close it.

3. CÉCILE:   I always have it open anyway.

4. SOPHIE:   Oh, I don't know how you can - I hate the thought of things flying in at night and hovering over my bed!

5. CÉCILE:   All part of life in the country! (PAUSE) I love it here, Sophie.

6. SOPHIE:   Yes. So you said at supper. And your 'friend' Alain confirmed, several times, that you belong here. But he's wrong!

7. CÉCILE:   Is he?

8. SOPHIE:   Definitely!

9. CÉCILE:   Are you sure you'll be all right on that fold-up bed?

10. SOPHIE: Yes. (THUMPS THE BED) It's a bit lumpy, but it's only for tonight.

1. CÉCILE: Sophie, listen to me. I want to live here.

2. SOPHIE: (PAUSE) I have listened, but when you talk it sounds like someone else - not my mother. Why do you suddenly want to hurt me?

3. CÉCILE: I don't.

4. SOPHIE: Then why do you want to get away from me, and why did you say those terrible things about Daddy?

5. CÉCILE: Yes, I'm sorry. I shouldn't have . . .

PAUSE

6. SOPHIE: It's all right. I know really that he wasn't perfect, but . . .

7. CÉCILE: He was to you - and that's what matters.

Oh, Sophie! I'm sorry!

8. SOPHIE: Mummy, you won't leave me, will you? I know I don't make much fuss of you - I'm too like Daddy, aren't I? But I do need you.

9. CÉCILE: I know.

10. SOPHIE: You wouldn't like living here on your own. You'd be lonely. Remember how you used to hate it when Daddy went away, or stayed out late. You used to say, as long as you had me, you were all right.

11. CÉCILE: Yes. (PAUSE) But couldn't I stay here for a while? You could visit me at weekends.

1. SOPHIE: No! Mummy, please. You can't leave me on my own in that flat. I nearly went crazy, when I was alone there before - you know I did.

2. CÉCILE: (DEFEATED) Yes.

3. SOPHIE: If you love me, you'll come back with me. You know I can't cope without you. (ATTEMPTS A LAUGH) I'm still your little girl.

4. CÉCILE: (IN TEARS) Yes. Yes.

5. SOPHIE: You're tired. We'll go to sleep now, Mother. And I think, really, I ought to take you home tomorrow. Now, turn off the light.

FX:   THE LIGHT IS SWITCHED OFF.
CÉCILE TOSSES AND TURNS. ONE BY
ONE BEES FLY IN THROUGH THE
WINDOW.

6. CÉCILE: (DREAMING, HALF AWAKE, ALMOST WHIMPERING) Oh, Sophie. No.

7. SOPHIE: (AS A CHILD) Mummy, please!

FX; THE BEES ARE SWARMING INTO THE
ROOM.

8. CÉCILE: (PLEADING) No!

9. SOPHIE: (IN THE DREAM) Oh, Mummy!

10. CÉCILE: (DREAMING) All right, Sophie. If you want me to.

FX:   THE SOUND OF THE BEES RISES
ALMOST TO A SCREAM.

1. SOPHIE: (AWAKE AND FRIGHTENED) Mother, wake up! Can you hear it?

2. CÉCILE: Yes.

3. SOPHIE: (GIVES A LITTLE SCREAM) Oh! Put the light on!

> FX: THE LIGHT CLICKS ON. SOPHIE SCREAMS IN TERROR AS BEES SURROUND HER.

4. CÉCILE: Oh, my God!

5. SOPHIE: Get them away! Get them away from me!

6. CÉCILE: Augustine!

> FX: AUGUSTINE'S VOICE CRIES THROUGH THE DEAFENING SOUND OF THE BEES

7. AUGUSTINE: (BITTER AND TEARFUL) 'Mother' they cry! Calling on you, calling on you all the time! You can never satisfy them! And they don't love you any more whatever you do!

   You listen to me! I know! You stay! You hear me now? You listen to me! You stay!

8. CÉCILE: Yes! Yes! I will! I'll stay.

## <u>SCENE 25.</u>

<u>FX: THE GARDEN. A BLACKBIRD SINGS
LOUDLY. IN THE DISTANCE A CAR BOOT
IS OPENED, CASES DUMPED INSIDE
AND THE BOOT SLAMMED SHUT.</u>

1. CÉCILE: (QUIETLY) It was her. A long black dress, and her hair tied at the back. Do you think I'm mad?

2. ALAIN: You saw what you saw. It must have been terrifying.

3. CÉCILE: Sophie's still shaky, but she's determined to drive back to Paris today. She was very upset this morning when I said I wouldn't go with her.

4. ALAIN: Well. (LAUGHS GENTLY) Children can't hang on to their parents for ever.

5. CÉCILE: No. It's like when you teach them to swim. You have to tell them you're letting go, or they'll never know the pleasure of slipping through the water on their own.

I think Sophie realises that she has to let go of me, too. But it's hard for her. The world isn't always a kind place to grow up in.

6. ALAIN: She'll come and see you. Learn to treasure you, perhaps.

7. CÉCILE: I hope so. She says she will go and talk to Philippe. She still loves him.

8. ALAIN: Do you think he'll still be waiting?

1. CÉCILE: (CERTAIN) Oh, yes.

      FX:   A FEW BEES BUZZ PAST THEM

2. ALAIN: Those damned bees are back. Over on the honeysuckle.

3. CÉCILE: Don't curse them, they're my friends. Oh, Alain, I feel so happy - and so guilty about it!

      SOPHIE APPROACHES.

4. SOPHIE: (FORMAL) Goodbye, M. Mercier. Goodbye, Mother.

5. CÉCILE: Oh, Sophie!

6. SOPHIE: (TRYING TO CONTROL HER EMOTIONS) Beautiful day, isn't it? (FALTERS) Your pansies seem to be turning their faces up to the sun.

7. CÉCILE: Yes.

8. SOPHIE: (GENTLY) It's all right, Mother. You're allowed to look happy. When I'm choking on the cigarette smoke in a meeting, I'll think of you out here, smiling in your garden.

9. CÉCILE: Thank you.

      FX:   THEY WALK TO THE CAR. SOPHIE OPENS THE CAR DOOR.

10. SOPHIE: Take care of her, M. Mercier. Goodbye, Mummy! (KISSES HER)

11. CÉCILE: Goodbye, love.

      FX:   SOPHIE GETS INTO THE CAR AND DRIVES AWAY.

1. ALAIN: Now, you stay out here and enjoy the sunshine, while I make us some lunch.

2. CÉCILE: No, I'll do it.

3. ALAIN: You heard what your daughter told me. I'm to take care of you!

4. CÉCILE: (PAUSE) No, Alain.

5. ALAIN: (GENTLE) It's all right. Only when you want me to. I won't make demands on you - or ask you to be grateful. But we can be 'together', can't we?

6. CÉCILE: Yes. (PAUSE) Will you call me, when it's ready? I'd like to go and sit in the orchard for a while - with my honeybees.

# SCENE 26.

FX:   THE ORCHARD. CÉCILE'S FOOTSTEPS IN THE GRASS. BIRDS SINGING. BEES.

# MADAME

by

## Liz Wainwright

Original Production
Directed by Marilyn Imrie
BBC Radio 4 Drama
Broadcast 1990
Running Time: 55m

Cast:

| | |
|---|---|
| Mme. Bernay | Mary Wimbush |
| Mlle. Rozier | Carole Boyd |
| Chantal/ Child/ Stallholder | Elaine Claxton |
| Marie-Louise/Woman | Elizabeth Kelly |
| M. Magrguier/ M. Chaumier/ Driver 1 | David King |
| Postman/ Workman 2/ M. Varescon | Danny Schiller |
| M. Duurand/ Driver 2 | Christopher Good |
| Italian Delivery Boy/ Workman 2 | Ben Onwukwe |

## SCENE 1 PROLOGUE.

F/X FRANTIC SCRATCHING SOUND LIKE A BIRD TRYING TO SCRABBLE OUT OF A CARDBOARD BOX. PAUSE. TITLES.

IN THE DISTANCE WE HEAR HORNS RAPIDLY SOUNDED,A WHISTLE IS BLOWN, DRIVERS EXPRESS THEIR IMPATIENCE.

1. DRIVERS: Allez-y! Allez-y, Madame! Oh, qu'est-ce qu'elle fait, la bagnole?

Oui, Monsieur! Moi aussi, je vais au bureau!

Un ban pour lui, uh?

IN THE NEAR DISTANCE HEAVY FOOTSTEPS AS TWO MEN PASS EACH OTHER. THROUGH AN OPEN WINDOW WE HEAR MUSIC ON THE RADIO. A WOMAN CALLS TO HER CHILD DOWN IN THE STREET.

2. WORKMAN 1:     Bonjour, Jean! Tu arrives de bonne heure ce matin!

3. WORKMAN 2:     Mais, oui!

4. WOMAN:  Vincent! Qu'est ce que tu fabriques la?

5. CHILD:    Rien, Maman!

## **SCENE 2.**

CLOSE TO THE MIC A TILED FLOOR
BEING SWEPT,THEN THE BUZZ OF THE
DOORBELL.

1. POSTMAN:   Bonjour, Madame Bernay!

2. MME BERNAY:   (SWEEPING THE TILED HALLWAY)
Bonjour, Monsieur.

3. POSTMAN:   Still keeping the place clean, I see!

4. MME BERNAY:   (APPROACHING) Yes, but not for much
longer. These 'apartments' should have
collapsed years ago - and me with them!

5. POSTMAN:   Now, don't talk like that! There's three letters
here, and one of them's for you!

6. MME BERNAY:   For me? Now who would be writing to an
old has- been like me?

PAUSE. WE HEAR HER SIT DOWN IN A
WICKER CHAIR IN THE DOORWAY. IN
THE FAR DISTANCE WE HEAR TRAFFIC
AND CLOSER A MOTOR CYCLE WHIRRS
PAST AND PEOPLE HURRY TO WORK.

7. MME BERNAY:   It's from Chantal! You'd think she would
have forgotten an old crow like me by now! But,
no, not my little Chantal!

WE HEAR THE RUSTLE OF PAPER AS
SHE READS THE LETTER, INTERRUPTED
BY THE OCCASIONAL GREETING AS
SOMEONE PASSES.

1. M. CHAUMIER:   Bonjour, Madame Bernay!

2. MME BERNAY:   Bonjour, Monsieur Chaumier!

3. CHANTAL:V.O.(AGED 43. WRITING) Marie- Claire is
      sixteen now! Almost a young woman -

4. MME BERNAY:   Yes! And, if she's as pretty as you were,
      Chantal, the boys will be after her!

> CHILDREN PASS BY ON THEIR WAY TO
> SCHOOL.

5. CHILDREN:   Bonjour, Madame!

6. MME BERNAY:   Bonjour! Michel, leave him alone - he's
      smaller than you!

7. CHANTAL:V.O.(WRITING) She wants to leave school , but
      I've said no. I want her to have her chance in
      life. I've told her that everyone should have that
      at least. You know what I mean, don't you,
      Tante Yvette?

8. MME BERNAY:   (SIGHS) Yes, I know. We don't forget, do
      we, you and I? You had your chance, when you
      were seventeen, didn't you, my pet, - almost!
      (PAUSE) When was it? (PAUSE) Over twenty
      years ago now, it must be. '63? '64? It was
      before the riots in 1968, I know that. I'd been
      concierge here for about ten years.

> F/X PAUSE. MME BERNAY'S VOICE IS
> HEARD AGAINST THE SOUND OF
> DISTANT FOOTSTEPS COMING FROM
> THE PAST. A DOOR IS LOCKED ON A
> LANDING AND THE FOOTSTEPS
> DESCEND THE STAIRS.

1. MME BERNAY:   Mlle. Rozier! I can hear her now, coming down the stairs in the morning. She always went to work after everyone else in the apartments. She claimed she suffered from claustrophobia so she couldn't possibly travel in the crush of bodies on the Metro at rush-hour!' So her boss allowed her to start work late - took it all in! Well, he was a man, he would!

2. MME BERNAY:   It used to go right through me every morning, those stupid high heels of hers scritch-scratching across the tiles in the hallway. The bitch!

   PAUSE. WE HEAR THE FOOTSTEPS APPROACHING.

3. MLLE ROZIER:   Bonjour, Madame!

4. MME BERNAY:   (PAST) Bonjour, Madame Rozier!

5. MLLE ROZIER:   I think your cat has been on my landing again, so perhaps you will be so kind as to use some disinfectant up there!

6. MME BERNAY:   I mopped the stairs and landings only yesterday!

7. MLLE ROZIER:   Really? One would never have guessed! Well, you need to do mine again. Today please! And keep that animal away from my door! Au revoir, Madame!

8. MME BERNAY:   Au revoir, 'Madame' Rozier!

   PAUSE.

1. MME BERNAY:   (PRESENT) (CHUCKLING) "Bonjour, 'Madame' Rozier! Au revoir,' Madame' Rozier!" I always used to shout for all to hear! It drove her up the wall! I knew that!

But everyone calls you Madame here when it's obvious you've passed a certain age, wedding ring or not! It's a courtesy! But she didn't see it that way. She refused to recognise her age! Insisted she was 'Mademoiselle' Rozier'! - even though she wouldn't see fifty again. She wasn't that much younger than me!

WE HEAR A CAT MIAOW.

Hello, Bobby! Come on, on my knee, pusskin!

(PAUSE)

She worked for Monsieur and Madame Durand in their little clothing business. I say little, but it was thriving at the time - making copies of all that English rubbish that was popular with the kids in the sixties.

WE HEAR THE CAT MIAOW AGAIN.

What's the matter? Want your breakfast do you? Come on then.

F/X (WE HEAR HER GET UP, SHUFFLE CARELESSLY INTO HER ROOM AT THE SIDE OF THE ENTRANCE TO THE BLOCK OF FLATS.)

1. MME BERNAY:   Yes, Bobby. The Durands were selling a lot of clothes in Paris in those days. Mlle boasted about it as if it was all her doing. Always going on about her flair for clothes. Pshaw! Anyone can dress well if they've got the money!

> WE HEAR HER OPEN A TIN AND SCRAPE
>
> FOOD INTO A DISH.

Here you are, greedy boy! And I'll have a cup of coffee while I read the rest of this letter from my Chantal.

> FILLS A PAN WITH WATER, LIGHTS THE
>
> GAS

She was mine, you know! Well, the nearest thing to a daughter that I ever had. We go back along way, her mother and I. Marie - Louise's husband was killed in the war, too, but she met Pierre later on. She always was desperate to be married!

> F/X (SHE PUTS A SPOONFUL OF COFFEE
>
> IN A CUP)

It was I who got Chantal the job at Durand's. I told Marie-Louise they would need more machinists, and that she should get Chantal to apply.

Mlle Rozier didn't like it, you know, when she found out, but there was nothing she could do about it by then because Chantal had already got the job.

## SCENE 3.

CUT TO DURAND'S SMALL CLOTHING
FACTORY. SEWING MACHINES WHIRR IN
THE BACKGROUND.

1. MLLE ROZIER:   (CLOSE TO THE MIC) I must confess, I was surprised you had employed that sort of girl, M. Durand.

2. M. DURAND: What do you, mean, Mlle Rozier?

3. MLLE ROZIER:   Well, her background. Her father is a cleaner on the Metro, and he drinks.

4. M.DURAND: Oh, dear! But that's not little Chantal's fault, is it?

5. MLLE ROZIER:   Oh, no, of course not. But these things have an effect on a person's character. You've taken a gamble there, you know, M. Durand. I wish you had spoken to me first.

6. M.DURAND: Yes. Perhaps I should have. (WHISPERS) But, as you know, there hasn't been the opportunity lately!

7. MLLE ROZIER:   No.

8. M. DURAND: Perhaps later this week?

9. MLLE ROZIER:   (COQUETTISH) Perhaps!

CUT TO:

## <u>SCENE 4.</u>

1. MME BERNAY:   (PRESENT) Chantal was thrilled to bits with the job, her imagination full of what it could lead to. And she had only been there a couple of months when it happened. I met her mother in the market .

> <u>F/X THE STREET MARKET. BOXES</u>
>
> <u>BEING STACKED AND EMPTIED OF</u>
>
> <u>PRODUCE. CRIES OF THE STALL-</u>
>
> <u>HOLDERS.</u>

2. STALLHOLDERS:    Deux kilos de pommes de terre, Madame! Et avec ca?/ Des oranges! Un franc soixante, ces oranges!/ Auhourd'hui j'ai des fromages de chèvre - très bon marché!

3. STALLHOLDER:  There you are, Madame, three kilos of apricots!

4. MME BERNAY:   You're making jam again, eh, Marie-Louise!

5. MARIE-LOUISE:  Oh, good morning, Yvette! Yes, Pierre loves his apricot jam for breakfast! I was just on my way to see you. I've some wonderful news! Chantal is going to be a model!

6. MME. BERNAY:  Is she?

7. MARIE-LOUISE:  Yes! The Durands are putting on a little show for some of their buyers - it's the first time they've done it - and Chantal is going to model the clothes for them! What do you think of that?

8. MME BERNAY:   Sounds too good to be true!

1. MARIE-LOUISE:  M. Durand asked her last night. I thought he liked her, you know. She said he's always smiling at her, and sometimes he pops a sweet on her desk as he's passing. It's become quite a little game!

2. MME. BERNAY:  Oh, yes? Well, as long as he doesn't think up any other 'little games'!

3. MARIE-LOUISE:  Oh, don't be silly, Yvette! You always think the worst of people!

4. MME BERNAY:  You don't know what I know!

5. MARIE-LOUISE:  It's her big chance, she knows that! She has the looks to be a model, hasn't she?

6. MME. BERNAY:  Of course she has! She's loveliness itself, that girl! (PAUSE) Oh, Marie- Louise! Who'd have thought that going to work for the Durands was going to lead to this.

   Chantal will have a better life than you or I could have dreamed of at her age! She won't end up like us now, thank God!

## **SCENE 5.**

1. MME BERNAY:  (PRESENT) A few days later I met Chantal coming out of the Metro. I'd nipped out to get a bottle of wine. I was in one of my remembering moods that day, and I knew I was in for a bad night, and that a drink might help.

> F/X TRAFFIC PASSING ON A BUSY
>
> STREET. DISTANT RUMBLE OF A TRAIN.
>
> IT IS RAINING. FOOTSTEPS COMING UP
>
> STEPS OUT OF THE METRO.

Chantal! What's the matter, child? You look as if Death's linked arms with you!

2. CHANTAL:  Oh, Tante Yvette! Hello, how are you?

3. MME BERNAY:  Never mind about me! Are you ill? Is that why you haven't been to see me? I was expecting you to come and tell me all about this modelling.

4. CHANTAL:  They don't want me to do it now! M. Durand has changed his mind.

5. MME BERNAY:  Why ?

6. CHANTAL:I don't know! I saw them talking in the office, Mme Durand and Mlle Rozier. I don't know what Mlle Rozier was telling her, but Mme Durand kept glancing at me, and started to look angry. Then the two of them went to talk to M. Durand.

7. MME BERNAY:  Oh, yes.

1. CHANTAL:    And then M. Durand came to see me and
said that they had decided to hire a professional
model instead - to give a better impression to
the clients. And that was it! Oh, Yvette, it was
my one chance! I'll never have that sort of
chance again!

2. MME BERNAY:    Of course you will! You're young! Plenty
of opportunities can come your way yet!

3. CHANTAL:No. I don't think so. I have that feeling about it.
Goodnight!

PAUSE. FADE OUT THE TRAFFIC ETC.

4. MME BERNAY:    (PRESENT) And she was right, of course.
She tried for about a year to get a modelling job
but there were hundreds of girls trying all ways
to get into the magazines in the sixties.

That was the only time a door opened for
Chantal, and I knew who had slammed it in her
face.

(TO THE CAT) We guessed what had happened
straight away, didn't we, Bobby? Mademoiselle
Rozier! The mean cow!

She couldn't even let an innocent child have a
bit of the limelight, the jealous bitch! Nobody
had to have anything except her. She thought
she was so superior to the rest of us poor
women. Just because she had managed to get
her grasping claws on some money - And how
did she get her money, hey? Ask her that and
see her shift her eyes!

(PAUSE)

1. MME BERNAY:   I think it was then I began to hate her.

    (PAUSE)

    Marie-Louise came to see me a few days later. She was still a bit upset for Chantal, but she was prepared to accept it. Well, that's Marie-Louise! She's the sort who's been brought up on pot-au-feu, and wouldn't think of even looking at the rump steak in the butcher's window!

2. MARIE-LOUISE: Have you seen Chantal lately, Yvette?

3. MME BERNAY:   (PAST) Yes, she called in yesterday to see if I wanted anything from town. Off on one of her trips round the Galerie Lafayette I think.

4. MARIE -LOUISE: Yes. She spends hours in the department stores just looking at the clothes.

5. MME BERNAY:   She doesn't seem well, she's so pale and quiet.

6. MARIE-LOUISE: Well, what can you expect when she doesn't sleep and can't be bothered to eat properly! I've told her! It's no good carrying on like that. All right, she's had a disappointment! But you can't always have what you want in life. You just have to accept it!

7. MME BERNAY:   Why? Other people grab what they want, and say to hell with anyone else! I've told Chantal to keep trying, look for other opportunities. She'll show the Durands and their broken promises!

8. MARIE-LOUISE: Oh, don't talk like that to Chantal or there'll be even more trouble. The sooner it's all forgotten about the better!

1. MME BERNAY:   No, Marie-Louise! She mustn't give up! You and I did that, and look at us!

2. MARIE-LOUISE: Oh, stop saying things like that! (PAUSE)I told her, she's still got her job. And there's some good come out of all this fuss. At least Mlle Rozier is being nice to her now.

3. MME BERNAY:   Hah! Is she?

4. MARIE-LOUISE: Oh yes, she speaks to her quite often now. Chantal doesn't like her, . . .

5. MME BERNAY:   (INTERRUPTS) I'm glad to hear it!

6. MARIE-LOUISE:  . . . but I've told her not to be so silly. It sounds to me as if Mlle Rozier is very well thought of at the Durands', she seems to almost run the place. It will do Chantal no harm to get well in with her.

PAUSE.

7. MME BERNAY:   (PRESENT) Oh, Marie-Louise! What an innocent! Of course Mlle was well thought of at Durand's, and I knew why! Where's that bottle of wine?

F/X (SHE POURS A GLASS OF WINE)

(DRINKING) I wasn't supposed to say anything. When I got this job Monsieur Marguier, the landlord, made it very clear that he didn't want to know about his tenants, as long as they paid their rent and didn't complain about things.

(TO THE CAT) No, we have to sit by this little window and pretend we notice nothing, don't we, Bobby? All right, you can have a drop of milk!

F/X (WE HEAR HER SHUFFLING ABOUT,
POURING MILK ETC. THE CAT
DRINKING).

1. MME BERNAY:   There wasn't much I didn't know about Mlle Rozier! Especially when I used to do her cleaning. Don't drink so fast, Bobby, that's all you're getting! She wouldn't give me a key. Couldn't trust me to be in there on my own! So I had to clean for her on Saturday mornings, with her standing there smoking her cigarettes, and watching me through those half closed venomous eyes.

2. MLLE ROZIER:   I think you'll have to do the parquet again, Madame, when you've finished dusting - there's still some fluff along the edges.

3. MME BERNAY:   (DUSTING PHOTO FRAMES) If you say so, Madame!

4. MLLE ROZIER:   Be careful with those photographs, they are very precious to me. You see that one you're holding, that's me on the steps of the Opera -a press photographer took it.

MME BERNAY CARRIES ON WITH HER
DUSTING.

5. MLLE ROZIER:   And that one - that's on the beach at Rimini. See the yacht anchored over there. Isn't she beautiful?

6. MME BERNAY:   I can't think of things like yachts as being beautiful. A child, yes, a child is beautiful.

1. MLLE ROZIER:   Well, I suppose I couldn't expect you to appreciate . . .

2. MME BERNAY:   Who are the men on the beach with you?

3. MLLE ROZIER:   Aah, that would be telling! Don't forget to dust the rubber plant, but gently!. I'm going to make my lunch now.

4. MME BERNAY:   (MUTTERING) Her and her plants, like a flaming greenhouse in here - ' . . plants give style, Mme Bernay, surely even you can see that!' Pretentious bitch!

F/X (SOUNDS OF FURNITURE BEING

SHOVED TO ONE SIDE AS SHE DUSTS)

5. MME BERNAY:   Wasn't going to tell me who her Italian men friends were, was she? Look at this place! Getting to be a real dump, time it had a coat of paint and some new covers at least! Where are your rich friends now Mademoiselle, eh?

WE HEAR A SCREAM FROM THE

KITCHEN AND MLLE ROZIER RUNNING

TOWARDS THE LIVING ROOM.

6. MLLE ROZIER:   (APPROACHING) Mme Bernay!

7. MME BERNAY:   What is it, Madame?

8. MLLE ROZIER:   (BRUSHING NERVOUSLY AT HER HAND) There's a spider in the kitchen cupboard. I was getting a saucepan and it ran across my hand!

9. MME BERNAY:   Well, that's nothing.

10. MLLE ROZIER:  Get rid of it for me, please! Get rid of it!

1. MME BERNAY:   All right! All right! (WALKS SLOWLY TO THE KITCHEN) They're quite harmless you know. I quite like them myself.

F/X (PAUSE. WE HEAR A THUMP FROM

THE KITCHEN)

(DISTANT) Sorry, fella, but Madame didn't want you here.

F/X SHE WALKS SLOWLY BACK INTO

THE LIVING ROOM

2. MLLE ROZIER:   Thank you.

3. MME BERNAY:   Don't mention it! Here he is. Quite a big fella, isn't he? Look at the size of it's body! Still twitching!

4. MLLE ROZIER:   (SCREAMING AND BECOMING ALMOST HYSTERICAL AS MME BERNAY HOLDS OUT THE SPIDER FOR HER INSPECTION) Take it away!

5. MME BERNAY:   F/X Calm yourself, Madame! (OPENS A WINDOW) There he goes - make a nice snack for some bird!(CLOSES THE WINDOW)

6. MLLE ROZIER:   (TRYING TO REGAIN HER DIGNITY) I'm sorry. I shouldn't have made such a fuss. But I'm afraid I have a morbid fear of the things. My mother locked me in a shed infested with them once -by accident, of course. Pass my cigarettes, will you?

F/X CIGARETTES PASSED OVER. MLLE

LIGHTS ONE.

1. MLLE ROZIER:   Terrible, isn't it, how one little incident can leave you with a fear like that? Of course, she didn't mean to do it. She was a very beautiful woman, my mother, tall and slim like me. I adored her. One of her friends had arrived, you see - a charming man -and we were playing a game, hide and seek, I suppose - and she forgot where I was! (LAUGHS)

2. MME BERNAY:   Can I do the bedroom now?

3. MLLE ROZIER:   Oh, yes. I'll just sit here a moment.

## SCENE 6.

### F/X THE CONCIERGE'S ROOM, HEAVY RAIN OUTSIDE.

1. MME BERNAY:   (PRESENT) It wasn't long after that she told me she no longer wanted me to clean for her.  1967 that was. I remember exactly because I was sixty that year and worried sick M. Marguier would get rid of me as soon as I reached my birthday. I couldn't believe that he'd keep me on like he has done.

Anyway. Mademoiselle had decided 'to make other arrangements' What she meant was, she couldn't afford to pay me any more!

(PAUSE) Still chucking it down! Enough to drive you daft this job, especially in this weather. (PAUSE) She was quite glad in a way, I think, to 'dispense with my services' as she put it. Never really liked me getting the chance to walk into her rooms, see how she lived.

(LAUGHS) Stupid woman! I had a key! The patron gave me a key to every flat. Swore to the tenants that only he had one, but like he said, if there was an emergency I had to be able to get in.

It was on the clear understanding that it was only to be used in emergencies - of course! But I used to get bored. So sometimes I used to have a wander round. Look at photographs, trinket boxes. Just to pass the time on a wet day.

(CONTINUED)

1. MME BERNAY:   She had some very interesting bits and pieces in her little boxes. A medal, uniform buttons, badges - quite an international collection, French, Italian, English, and German - but no Russian. I suppose even she had to draw the line somewhere!

   So I didn't miss anything when she stopped my cleaning job. Except the money, of course, I could have done with that.

   It rained a lot that summer as well, if I remember rightly. Thank god Marie- Louise still came to see me!

   > F/X WE HEAR A TAP ON THE WINDOW
   >
   > ABOVE THE SOUND OF THE RAIN
   >
   > RATTLING AGAINST IT.

2. MARIE-LOUISE: Yvette! Yvette!

3. MME BERNAY:   (PAST) (WAKING UP) What? Oh, Marie-Louise. Just a minute.

   > F/X (SHE PRESSES A BUTTON, A
   >
   > BUZZER SOUNDS AND THE OUTER
   >
   > DOOR OPENS MARIE-LOUISE ENTERS,
   >
   > PAUSES TO SHAKE HER UMBRELLA INTO
   >
   > THE HALLWAY)

4. MARIE-LOUISE: I couldn't make you hear me.(GIVES THE UMBRELLA A FINAL SHAKE) It's pouring down! Will my umbrella be all right left in the hall, do you think?

5. MME BERNAY:   Yes! Take your coat off. I'll make us a drink. Tea all right? I've run out of coffee.

1. MARIE-LOUISE: Yes. Lovely! How are you?

2. MME BERNAY:   How are you supposed to be when you're sixty next birthday and life's passed you by?

3. MARIE-LOUISE: Oh, Yvette. Cheer up! I've brought you some good news. Chantal's going to have a baby!

4. MME BERNAY:   (MAKING TEA) Already? She and what's his name, Alain, have only been married a year!

5. MARIE-LOUISE: Well, that's time enough! Aren't you pleased?

6. MME BERNAY:   No.

7. MARIE-LOUISE: Of course you are! And she's coming to see us in August - when Alain has a few days holiday. And I expect she'll want to come and see her Aunty Yvette. You'll like that, won't you?

8. MME BERNAY:   Stop humouring me as if I were an old woman! I'm not past it yet, you know! (PAUSE) Yes, I would like to see her. My poor little Chantal!

9. MARIE-LOUISE: She's not 'poor little Chantal' - she's happy!

10. MME BERNAY: You think so? She didn't want that! She never wanted that! Stuck in Lille scratching a living and having babies!

11. MARIE-LOUISE:   Oh, I wish I hadn't come! You're in one of your moods, I can see that! I'll go if you like!

12. MME BERNAY: No, no, I'm sorry! I just feel old today, that's all. And caged up in this place!

1. MARIE-LOUISE: F/X You ought to count your blessings! (SHOWS HER A NEWSPAPER) You talk about being caged up. Look at these poor devils in the newspaper! Put in a cage while they await trial! They look like stray dogs waiting to be put down! It's indecent!

<u>F/X RATTLE OF CUPS PLACED ON A</u>

<u>TABLE, A CHAIR IS DRAWN UP.</u>

2. MME BERNAY: It's in Italy that. They're members of the Mafia!

3. MARIE-LOUISE: Yes, but whoever they are, I can't bear to see pictures of faces like that.

4. MME BERNAY: They deserve all they get! They kill and torture as if it's a game. They assume they can take what they want from life just because they want it! They think they're special! (PAUSE)Like her!

5. MARIE-LOUISE: Who?

6. MME BERNAY: Mademoiselle! She thinks she's special, and that she has a right to have just what she wants!

7. MARIE-LOUISE: Yes, but she's not a criminal, you can't compare her with the Mafiosi.

8. MME BERNAY: It's the same principle! Always putting yourself first, and not caring about how you get what you want, as long as you get it!

All right, it's on a much smaller scale, what she does, but it can harm people just the same!

1. MARIE-LOUISE: You go too far, Yvette! Who has Mlle Rozier harmed?

2. MME BERNAY: You ask me that? Chantal, your own daughter for a start!

3. MARIE-LOUISE: Oh, that was all a long time ago. You say it was her fault, but you can't prove anything.

4. MME BERNAY: I don't need to prove. I know! And look at the harm that caused! Look at what's happened to Chantal! Married to a good for nothing!

5. MARIE-LOUISE: Alain is all right. He's not a great catch, but he's well-meaning, and very good-looking! And he was Chantal's choice.

6. MME BERNAY: Yes, but you helped her to choose, with your obsession with weddings and engagement presents! And what real choices did she have in her life?

   She tried for what she wanted, but there were too many other girls after those jobs. And she was too good to take the dirty way.

   Not like Mademoiselle with her 'visitors' to her apartment upstairs!

7. MARIE-LOUISE: Ssh! I've told you before, you shouldn't talk like that!

8. MME BERNAY: Oh, come on, Marie-Louise! How else do you think she got clothes like she wears, and the jewellery!

9. MARIE-LOUISE: I don't know.

10. MME BERNAY: Well I do! Makes you ashamed to be a woman! I wouldn't take advantage of the poor creatures with their hungry bodies like she does - though I've had offers enough, haven't I, Marie-Louise?

1. MARIE-LOUISE: Oh, yes. You were always a fine looking woman, Yvette - still are!

2. MME BERNAY:  It's pitiful to watch them creeping up the stairs behind her.

3. MARIE-LOUISE: She doesn't still have . . men friends?

4. MME BERNAY:  Of course she does! She won't give it up as long as she can still find a man to give her money.

5. MARIE-LOUISE: But she's fifty two, at least, you told me!

6. MME BERNAY:  I know! It's obscene! You and I know how to behave at our age, but not her!

7. MARIE-LOUISE: Oh, Yvette, it's horrible! Does she need the money that badly?

8. MME BERNAY:  She's a whore, carrying on just the same as she's always done! The only difference is the men are getting older, and can't get up the stairs as often! So she's having to cut back a little, like not paying me any more.

9. MARIE-LOUISE: How awful! She must be desperate.

10. MME BERNAY: Don't waste your sympathy on her! She's had more than you and I have ever had! Even during the war she did all right for herself. .

11. MARIE-LOUISE:  How do you know? You're making things up now, Yvette!

12. MME BERNAY: No, I'm not! She tells me bits about herself when she feels like showing off and needs an audience. She travelled around a lot in the war, likes to make out she was in the Resistance - but who knows? Sounds like the Black Market was more in her line. She never queued for half a loaf of bread like we did.

1. MARIE-LOUISE:  Oh, what times those were, Yvette! I know it's a terrible thing to say, but sometimes I wish. . . . (PAUSE) at least we knew how to be happy in those days.

2. MME BERNAY:  We were a lot younger then. (PAUSE) Robert and I were still trying for a baby when . ..(PAUSE)

3. MARIE-LOUISE:  (GENTLY) I know.

4. MME BERNAY:  She didn't stay in Paris once things started to get rough, though. Flew off down to Nice with the rest of the butterflies!

5. MARIE-LOUISE:  While we stayed here to starve and have nightmares about the Germans coming to get us.

6. MME BERNAY:  Yes! Later she went on to Italy. She clams up as soon as she starts to talk about that, though, but there are photos and things in her room. Mademoiselle had a good time in Italy - she boasted once that she still has influential friends there!

7. MARIE-LOUISE:  Oh!

8. MME BERNAY:  It might be true - she had a letter from Rome a few days ago. I asked her for the stamps but she wouldn't give them to me. But it makes you sick, seeing people like her taking, taking all the time while we have to make do with all the scraps life dishes out!

9. MARIE-LOUISE:  I know. It's not fair. (PAUSE) But we haven't done too badly, at least, I haven't. I know it's different for you because you lost Robert.

10. MME BERNAY: Yes.

1. MARIE-LOUISE: But you could have married again, after the war. I never understood why you didn't.

2. MME BERNAY:   (PAUSE) I'd known Robert, so I knew how good a man could be. I wanted no other.

3. MARIE-LOUISE: But it's not easy for a woman on her own. You could have done with someone to look after you.

4. MME BERNAY:   I've been tempted, but I could give nothing in return to a man who wanted me. I don't take advantage of the weak - not like Mlle Rozier, sucking her happiness out of other people's lives!

5. MARIE-LOUISE: You're too hard on her, Yvette. Everyone deserves a little pity!

6. MME BERNAY:   She doesn't! She's a parasite, taking up space that could be given to others! She ought to be done away with!

7. MARIE-LOUISE: Oh, you mustn't say things like that! (PAUSE) Let's get out your box of photos and remember the good times, eh?

## SCENE 7.

1. MME BERNAY:   (PRESENT) A few weeks later
Mademoiselle and I had a row. A real up and
downer! I quite enjoyed it except for the fact that
the bitch nearly had me sacked.  It was hot.
Most of the tenants had gone away for the
summer. I sat outside whenever I could.

2. M. VARESCON:   Good evening, Mme Bernay. Would you
like my newspaper?

3. MME BERNAY:   If you've finished with it, thank you, M
Varescon. Off to join your wife in Deauville
tomorrow, aren't you?

4. M. VARESCON:   Yes, and I'll be very grateful if you would
keep my mail for me.

5. MME BERNAY:   Of course.

6. M. VARESCON:   And that's for you.

7. MME BERNAY:   Oh, thank you very much, Monsieur.

8. M. VARESCON:   I wish you a pleasant evening, Madame!

PAUSE.

1. MME BERNAY:   Must be nice to go off to the coast, eh, Bobby. Ah, well! Now what's happening in the world today? (LEAFS THROUGH THE PAPER) Tour de France. Agricultural policy. Sex scandal in Neuilly. (PAUSE) (READS) 'Mafia. Who dares to testify?' Huh! They thought they had him, the old Mafioso! Looks like he's getting away again, though.

(READS) 'No-one dares to breach omerta, the Mafia's rule of silence. So far the police have failed to find anyone willing to give evidence against the old Mafia boss, Spiro, known as the Stone Man.' Pathetic! (READS) Still hoping for witnesses to come forward.' It only takes one to tell, doesn't it, Bobby? Oh, look at that face!

> F/X PAUSE. A TAXI DRAWS UP OUTSIDE
>
> THE BUILDING.

2. MLLE ROZIER:   (DISTANT) That's all right, you can keep the change. If you'd just pass me that other parcel. Thank you.

> THE CAR DOOR IS SLAMMED, AND WE
>
> HEAR MLLE APPROACHING, CARRYING
>
> PARCELS.

3. MLLE ROZIER:   Good evening, Madame Bernay! Sunning yourself out here as usual! All right for some! My office has been unbearable today in this heat! (SHE STRUGGLES WITH HER PARCELS, TRYING TO GET HER KEY OUT OF HER HANDBAG) Would you mind holding some of these parcels for a moment while I find my key?

4. MME BERNAY:   (PAST) Been having a spending spree, Madame?

1. MLLE ROZIER:   Just one or two dresses and a few treats. Now that that dreadful rain has stopped one needs to have clothes that are comfortable in this heat.

2. MME BERNAY:   If you can afford them! Had a pay rise have you, Madame?

3. MLLE ROZIER:   Not that it's any of your business, but yes I have had, what shall we say, a slight change of fortune.

(SHE FINDS HER KEY AND RETRIEVES

HER PARCELS)

My parcels please. (PARCELS PASSED OVER) Thank you, Madame. And I think you might sweep the pavement a little. I'm sure when M. Marguier comes on his monthly visit, he wouldn't like to hear that his tenants had dirt and swarms of flies to walk through before they can enter the building!

F/X WE HEAR HER HIGH HEELED

FOOTSTEPS SCRATCHING ACROSS THE

HALLWAY AND UP THE STAIRS.

4. MME BERNAY:   (MUTTERING TO HERSELF) Ha! How would she like to sweep up dog dirt in this heat? Is it my fault the place is infested with flies?

(SHE WALKS INTO HER ROOM)

All right for some, she says! It certainly is! Buying this and buying that. I don't know where she's getting the money from all of a sudden, but she's certainly living well. A leg of lamb she bought last week, the butcher told me! There's something going on. I don't know what it is, but I'll find out.

## SCENE 8.

F/X FADE UP MME BERNAY GOING
UPSTAIRS AND QUIETLY UNLOCKING
THE DOOR OF THE FLAT. AS THE DOOR
OPENS WE HEAR SEVERAL FLIES
BUZZING AROUND. THE CAT MIAOWS.

1. MME BERNAY: Ssh, Bobby! Phew! It's hot in here. And it stinks! Bet she hasn't cleaned it since she'd dispensed with my services'. Now where shall we start? The bedroom.

F/X WE HEAR HER WALK THROUGH THE
HALLWAY AND ENTER THE BEDROOM.
SILENCE.

Huh! Not even made her bed this morning! Yes, all right, you curl up on there if you like, she won't notice a few hairs!

F/X SHE WALKS OVER TO THE
WARDROBE AND OPENS IT.

Let's have a look in here and see what clothes she bought herself yesterday. (SLIDING THE CLOTHES ALONG THE RAIL) Mmm three new dresses, I reckon! Not cheap either by the look of it.

Oh, feel this one, Bobby! Oh, to wear a dress that feels like this. Look! (PAUSE) Robert would have loved me in this. (PAUSE) All right, Bobby, don't blink at me like that - I'm just a foolish old woman! (SHE CLOSES THE WARDROBE)

F/X (SHE OPENS DRAWERS AND
CLOSES THEM)

1. MME BERNAY:   New underwear, as well! (PAUSE AS SHE
RUMMAGES) Nothing under here.

Too clever to hide her secrets in her underwear
drawer like most women, the old cow! But we
know where she hides them, don't we, Bobby?
Under the gramophone. Come on; let's take a
look.

F/X (SHE WALKS INTO THE LIVING

ROOM. HERE THE FLIES ARE MORE

NUMEROUS AND NOISY. WE HEAR THEM

BANGING AGAINST THE WINDOW PANE.)

Huh! Look at the dust! (SHE KNEELS ON THE
FLOOR) Now let's see what's in the old cigar
box, shall we? F/X (COUNTING NOTES ) Eight
hundred franc notes! Do you think she'd miss
one, Bobby? (SIGHS) I suppose she would. F/X
(SHE SIFTS THROUGH PAPERS)

What else is there? Receipts for all the clothes
she's been buying. And here are those letters
she's had from Italy. (SHE TAKES ONE OUT OF
ITS ENVELOPE) Perhaps they're from an old
flame.

Must be desperate if he fancies her skinny,
dried up body! And the make-up doesn't help
any more either, however much she plasters it
on!

(PAUSE)

1. MME BERNAY:   Hmm. doesn't believe in writing long letters, does he? (PAUSE) It's all in bloody Italian, Bobby! How am I expected to read this?

<u>F/X (PUSHES THE LETTER BACK IN ITS ENVELOPE)</u>

God, it's hot in here. Like the flaming jungle with all these plants and the flies crawling all over them. Makes you thirsty. Wonder if there's anything in the drinks cupboard. Still the same old dregs, I suppose. F/X (SHE OPENS A CUPBOARD DOOR) No, I beg her pardon! A new bottle of brandy! Well, well! Let's sit down a minute, shall we?

(UNSCREWS THE TOP) Won't miss a little drop, will she? Cheers, Bobby!

(PAUSE) Look at these photos! Men, men, men! Hardly another woman to be seen, except that one of her mother. Look at those eyes and that mouth! I bet she liked the men, too! F/X (PICKS UP PHOTOS AND PUTS THEM DOWN AGAIN) Look at this fella in R.A.F. uniform. Fancied themselves did the RAF! Kept the Résistance busy picking them up after they'd ditched their planes. The ones you could pick up!

Too many young men, Bobby. Some survived of course. The question is, were they the right ones? Look at these, with her and her Italian beach boyfriend. He looks like the type who would survive - one way or another! (PAUSE) I know that face. (PAUSE) Huh! Dusted it often enough, I should do! Come on, out we go, Bobby. Better put the bottle back. Mademoiselle has a suspicious mind!

<u>PAUSE.</u>

1. MME BERNAY:   (PRESENT) I don't know how she knew I'd been in there, but she did!

2. MLLE ROZIER:   Mme Bernay! I wish to speak to you!

3. MME BERNAY:   (PAST) Yes, Madame?

4. MLLE ROZIER:   Someone has been in my room!

5. MME BERNAY:   Are you sure, Madame? I have seen no one, and I am on watch here most of the day, you know that. Has anything been stolen?

6. MLLE ROZIER:   No. At least, I don't think so. But my privacy has been invaded, I can feel it! Oh, the signs are only small but they are there!

7. MME BERNAY:   What signs, Madame?

8. MLLE ROZIER:   Things have been moved. Someone has been sitting on the sofa, I can see from the cushions. And someone has drunk some of my brandy.

9. MME BERNAY:   Are you sure? Had you marked the bottle?

10. MLLE ROZIER:  Of course not.

11. MME BERNAY: Well, I'm sorry, Madame Rozier, but it sounds to me as if you are imagining things. You do, you know, as you get older.

12. MLLE ROZIER: Don't be insolent! (PAUSE) You have a key, haven't you?

13. MME BERNAY: Now you know very well, Madame, that only M. Marguier has a key to the apartments. And anyway, why would I want to go into your rooms?

1. MLLE ROZIER:   Because you like to look! You like to be nosey! Sitting here in your squalid little room, with that horrible cat. (PAUSE) I found some hairs on my sheet! Of course! They were cat hairs! It was you! (PAUSE) When M. Marguier comes tomorrow I shall speak to him. If I were you I would start looking for another place where you can rot with your filthy animal

CUT.

## SCENE 9.

1. M. MARGUIER:   But you say nothing is missing, Mlle Rozier. And you have no real proof that anyone was in your apartment.

2. MLLE ROZIER:   She was in there! I know she was! I've complained to you before about her, haven't I, M. Marguier. You must know the kind of woman she is!

3. M. MARGUIER:   But why would Mme Bernay want to go into your apartment? As I said, nothing has been stolen.

4. MLLE ROZIER:   She would go in to look! To pry into my private possessions!

5. MME BERNAY:   M. Marguier, I assure you . . .

6. MLLE ROZIER:   I've caught her looking at my things when she used to clean for me - envy all over her face!

7. MME BERNAY:   Envy! Why should I envy you!

8. MLLE ROZIER:   Because that's the sort of person you are. And because you're old and ugly - not young enough to still have a life like I do! She reeks of envy and self-pity, M. Marguier!

9. M. MARGUIER:   Mlle, please we do not need to . . .

10. MLLE ROZIER: All she does is sit there and spy on other people's lives. She has never had the courage to make a life of her own. Not like me, M. Marguier. I, too, am a woman alone. It is not easy for me without a man to look after me.

1. M. MARGUIER:   Yes. Yes, I'm sure it isn't easy, Mlle.

2. MLLE ROZIER:   But I do not feel sorry for myself and skulk behind a curtain like she does. I have always made something of my life, tried to live it to the full!

3. MME BERNAY:   Oh, yes! But who has paid for it, hey? You have always looked at me with contempt in your eyes, Mademoiselle! But I would rather live honestly and respectably - whatever that brings me in life, than be an ageing whore like you!

(MLLE ROZIER SLAPS HER ACROSS THE FACE.)

4. M. MARGUIER:   Mme Bernay! Apologise at once! I will not hear you speak to one of my tenants in such a manner!

CUT

5. MME BERNAY:   (PRESENT) It always comes down to money in the end, doesn't it? She paid him a good rent, and if anyone moved out it wasn't so easy to find new tenants for such run down apartments. (PAUSE) So, he gave me a hard time, did Monsieur Marguier. We were scared, weren't we, Bobby? I mean, where could we have gone? (PAUSE) Ooh, that cow!

PAUSE.

1. MME BERNAY:  Anyway, we managed to stay. I told him about her 'gentleman callers' - on the quiet so she couldn't get me for slander - so that lost her a bit of his sympathy. But he made me hand over her key - and apologise to her for having it! While he stood there, all innocent! Who gave it to me in the first place? He took the other keys as well, later when she'd gone.

Mlle started to make my life a real misery after that, complaining, and making nasty remarks. She knew I had to watch my step now. So she felt she had some real power over me -the bitch!

F/X (SORTING THROUGH A BUNCH OF KEYS)

Time we locked up, Bobby.

F/X (CLOSES A LARGE DOOR AND LOCKS IT, THEN WALKS BACK ACROSS THE EMPTY HALLWAY AND CLOSES AND LOCKS THE DOOR TO HER ROOM)

She wouldn't have been so happy if she'd known how I'd outsmarted her, would she, Bobby? I'd guessed what would happen. So before M. Marguier arrived I nipped round to the ironmonger's and had a copy made of her key - just for the hell of it!

## SCENE 10.

1. MME BERNAY:   (PRESENT) I couldn't stand the way she was lording it over me! Making me jump whenever she could! It was made worse by the fact that all the other tenants had gone away, so there was only me and her in the building. The only thing I had to look forward to that August was Chantal's visit. But oh, when she came!

   I hardly recognised her. Hair all over the place, face pink and podgy, and her eyes – oh those empty eyes! I could have wept.

2. CHANTAL:Tante Yvette! It's lovely to see you again! (KISSES HER) How are you?

3. MME BERNAY:   Never mind me! What's happened to you, child?

4. CHANTAL:What do you mean? (LAUGHS) This great lump? But Maman told you I was expecting, didn't she?

5. MME BERNAY:   Yes. But . . .

6. CHANTAL:Not long to go now! Alain is so thrilled! But he's also scared to death! The silly man!

7. MME BERNAY:   You'd better come in out of this heat and sit down.

8. CHANTAL:Yes, I am ready for a sit down!

9. MME BERNAY:   (PRESENT) You should have seen the way she walked in and flopped down in my old chair -just like her mother does! She was bubbling over with the excitement, couldn't stop talking about it all. She must have thought I was going senile, the way I sat there at first - just staring at her with my mouth hanging open.

1. CHANTAL:   Oh, won't it be wonderful? A little baby to hold in my arms. I've been practising on my friend's little girl - and oh, when I put my cheek against her soft little head as it nudges into my shoulder - oh I could melt! And that's just someone else's baby! Imagine when it's your own!

2. MME BERNAY:   But how will you manage? Have you got enough money?

3. CHANTAL: Well, you know what it's like - you never have enough money, do you, especially when you're starting a family. But Alain should get a pay rise in September, and I can still do my sewing at home after the baby arrives.

4. MME BERNAY:   Are you managing to get everything you need for the baby?

5. CHANTAL: Oh, yes! Do you know, Alain's mother had saved his old cot all these years! Alain's painted it up and it looks so pretty. And we were ever so lucky with the pram - it's second-hand but there's hardly a scratch on it. It was a real bargain!

6. MME BERNAY:   (PRESENT) And so she went on, sounding more like Marie-Louise every minute. Accepting compromises and making out they were good fortune. I've never compromised like that!

7. CHANTAL: And how are things here. Are you and Mlle Rozier getting on any better?

8. MME BERNAY:   Why should I want to get on with her?

9. CHANTAL: Well you've both lived here a long time. And you're both on your own. It seems a shame you've never been friends. She must be lonely.

1. MME BERNAY:   She has her men friends! I never told you about that!

2. CHANTAL:Mother told me, about her 'gentleman callers'. It must be awful to have to go with men because you need money. And when you're as old as she is . . it's terrible.

3. MME BERNAY:   How can you squander your pity on her - after what she did to you? Ruining your life!

4. CHANTAL:What? Oh, you mean the modelling business. That might not have been her fault.

5. MME BERNAY:   Of course it was her fault! You don't know her like I do!

6. CHANTAL:No. But that's all in the past. And now I have Alain, and soon we'll have our baby. What more could I want?

7. MME BERNAY:   (PRESENT) It wasn't until she was going that I realised I had nothing to give her for the baby. Not even a few francs.

8. MME BERNAY:   I'd tried knitting a little coat but it looked so cheap and homemade, I threw it away in the end.  After she'd gone I sat down, and I cried. I haven't cried for years - not since  Robert.

   I think I cried with rage more than anything. Rage against her, that bitch, and what she'd done to my little Chantal.

9. MME BERNAY:   (PAST) Oh, Bobby, did you see her? Did you see my poor child and what has become of her?

   And I can't help her, I haven't a sou! That bitch robbed Chantal of her only chance in life, and there she is, Mlle Rozier! - spending money on finery for herself, and with hundred franc notes piled up in her box under the gramophone.

1. MME BERNAY:   I ought to go up there and take the lot to give to Chantal. It would only be part of what Mlle stole from her! And she couldn't prove anything. No one else knows about her hidden treasure. It would be her word against mine!

PAUSE, REPEAT THE SCRATCHING

SOUND HEARD AT THE BEGINNING OF

THE PLAY.

It was that afternoon that the plant arrived. Horrible looking thing! Thick wrinkled stem - obscene I called it - and fleshy long thin leaves with sharp points.

2. MME BERNAY:   'What the hell do you call this?' I asked the young lad who brought it. Not the usual sort of delivery boy you meet. He wore a suit and those fancy Italian leather shoes with all the stitching.

3. BOY:   It's a Yucca plant. They grow in South America. It's for Mlle. Rozier. She does live here, doesn't she?

4. MME BERNAY:   Yes, more's the pity!

5. BOY:   I have to see that this plant is delivered to her straight away.

6. MME BERNAY:   She'll be home from work in about half an hour. I'll give it to her as soon as she gets in. Ugly looking thing. They should go well together!'

7. BOY:   You are sure she will be here in half an hour.

9. MME BERNAY:   Yes. If not earlier! She's punctual, you can say that for her. And it's about all you can say!

1. BOY: I ought to wait to deliver it personally, but there is someone I have arranged to meet.

2. MME BERNAY: Oh, yes! A girl is it? All the same you men! Go on, you can leave it with me. I'll see that she gets it.

3. BOY: You will not forget. As soon as she comes in?

4. MME BERNAY: I won't forget.

5. BOY: May I give you this to remind you? (HANDS OVER A NOTE)

6. MME BERNAY: Thanks very much. Help my memory no end will that! Who's the plant from? Isn't there a card with it.

7. BOY: No, there is no card.

8. MME BERNAY: But she'll want to thank whoever sent it?

9. BOY: (TRIES NOT TO LAUGH) No, Madame. I do not think she will want to thank him. Goodbye, Madame!

(WE HEAR HIS LAUGHTER AS HE WALKS AWAY)

10 MME BERNAY: (PRESENT) I could hear him laughing all the way down the street. There was a big black Citroen waiting for him at the corner

It was a ten franc note he gave me! Whoever heard of a delivery boy who could hand out ten franc notes? I shoved the plant on the table by my door, where I put all the letters and parcels.

(PAUSE. SCRATCHING SOUND IS REPEATED)

1 MME BERNAY:   (PRESENT) I hardly bothered to look at the thing again till I was walking past it carrying a cup of coffee that had gone cold.

It was then I noticed that it needed watering. The soil was so dry that it had started to shrink away from the edge of the pot and from round the stem, leaving a couple of holes down the side. So I tipped the dregs of the coffee into it.

(SCRATCHING SOUND)

The soil swallowed it down so fast I hardly saw it go in!(PAUSE)

And then I heard this scratching noise. Quite loud and frantic for a minute, then it stopped.

I looked in the leaves but I couldn't see anything, so I thought I must have been hearing things.

I nearly went to get it some water because it was obviously desperate, but then I said to myself, 'Why the hell should I? It belongs to that bitch, why should I bother whether it lives or dies? She can water it herself!

I thought I heard that scratching noise again a little while later, like a frantic bird or something. I nearly took the plant upstairs to leave it outside her door, but it was too hot to go climbing stairs.

All the same I was glad to get rid of it when Mademoiselle came home. I remember she was wearing one of her new summer dresses, a short, thin, skimpy affair with no sleeves. A young girl's dress. Not one for an ageing whore like her!

F/X SCRATCHING SOUND. THEN MLLE

ROZIER'S FOOTSTEPS APPROACHING.

1. MME BERNAY:   (PAST) There's a plant here for you,
   Madame!

2. MLLE ROZIER:   A plant?

3. MME BERNAY:   That's what it looks like to me!

4. MLLE ROZIER:   Oh, a yucca plant! I haven't got one of
   those! Lovely! I wonder who it's from?

5. MME BERNAY:   I don't know, there's no card - not that I
   would have read it if there was! A young man
   brought it.

6. MLLE ROZIER:   Did he not say who sent it?

7. MME BERNAY:   No. He just said I was to make sure you
   got it straight away. Perhaps it's from one of
   your old admirers!

8. MLLE ROZIER:   Be careful, Madame Bernay! I pay rent,
   remember. You don't! (GOING UPSTAIRS) I
   think I'll stand it in front of the fireplace, it will
   hide the empty chimney nicely.

PAUSE. SCRATCHING SOUND

REPEATED. PAUSE.

9. MME BERNAY:   (PRESENT) It was about lunchtime when
   I called M. Marguier the next day.

1. MME BERNAY:   (PAST) (ON THE TELEPHONE) Yes, M. Marguier, I know you don't want to be called unless it's an emergency. . .

. . . Yes, I'm sure she hasn't come down. I've been here all morning, I would have seen her. And she never goes to work more than a quarter of an hour late

. . . . . That's why I didn't phone till now but it's almost one o'clock, no one sleeps in so long. . . . . . . Yes, I've banged on the door but there's no reply.

CUT.

## SCENE 11.

SCRATCHING SOUND IN THE

BACKGROUND. TWO PAIRS OF

FOOTSTEPS GO UP THE STAIRS.

1. M. MARGUIER:   (KNOCKING LOUDLY) Mlle Rozier? Are
you in? It's M. Marguier!

(KNOCKS AGAIN. PAUSE. A BUNCH OF

KEYS, THE DOOR IS OPENED. THE

SCRATCHING SOUND RISES TO A

CRESCENDO. SILENCE.)

2. M. MARGUIER:   Hello! Mlle Rozier! (THEY WALK
THROUGH THE HALL AND INTO THE LIVING
ROOM. FLIES BUZZ LOUDLY) Oh, God in
Heaven!

PAUSE.

3. MME BERNAY:   (PRESENT) She was lying there on the
floor in front of the hearth. Next to her,
surrounded by a damp stain, was the little
watering can she used for her plants.

Her body was twisted and stretched like apiece
of rotten driftwood. Her eyes were wide-open
and screaming, her teeth biting crookedly into
her bottom lip.

Her right arm was reaching out to us.

On her arm were two tiny red dots, but we
didn't notice them till the doctor pointed them
out later.

1. MME BERNAY:   We backed out of the room. As we walked through the hall I saw something move on the floor. It was a black spider with a fat shiny body.  M. Marguier crushed it under his thick-soled shoe. It lay on its back scrabbling with its long thin legs. On its belly there was a strange red mark, shaped a bit like an hourglass. He stamped on it again and it stopped twitching.

<u>PAUSE.</u>

The pathologist's report said it was a Black Widow spider, normally found in Australia and South America, so he assumed it must have somehow got into the plant pot. Its bite is fatal in only four per cent of cases, so he was of the opinion that Mlle Rozier's death had been caused by the heart attack she had suffered, rather than by the spider's poison.

But one couldn't be sure. Her body did show some symptoms associated with such a poison, and her heart appeared to have been quite strong for her age. (PAUSE) There was a serum available for the poison, if anyone could have reached her in time.

<u>PAUSE.</u>

No one had heard her screaming except me. But I could have done nothing about it. (PAUSE)

After all, I didn't have a key, did I?

# MRS DANBY'S DESTINY

by

Liz Wainwright

Original Production
Directed by Marion Nancarrow
BBC Radio 4 Drama
*'Thirty Minute Theatre'*
Broadcast November 1993
Running Time: 30m

Cast:
Susan    Pauline Yates
Greg    James Taylor
Julia    Lynda Baron

## **MUSIC:**

JACK JONES 'Wives and Lovers'

NAT KING COLE 'A Blossom Fell'

'Unforgettable'

HARRY SECOMBE 'Katharine'

FRANK SINATRA 'Come Fly With Me'

'It's all right with me'

'You're sensational' (High Society)

FRANKIE LANE 'Jezebel'

STRAUSS WALTZ 'Vienna Woods'

'Paper Roses'

## <u>SCENE 1.</u>

<u>KITCHEN OF A LARGE ECHOING HOUSE,
WINDOW RATTLES IN THE WIND.</u>

<u>A TAPE PLAYS:    WIVES AND LOVERS.</u>

<u>SUSAN CUTS UP SALAD INGREDIENTS,
MIXES DRESSING ETC, SINGING
WISTFULLY.</u>

1. GREG:     (ENTERING) Oh, not flaming salad again!

2. SUSAN:     It's good for you, and the doctor said . . . .

3. GREG:     I know what he said! (HE SWITCHES OFF THE TAPE)

4. SUSAN:     (TO HERSELF) Just like my Dad! Switching things off!

(TO GREG) Greg! Leave it on. Please.

5. GREG:     You can have it on when I've gone.

6. SUSAN:     You're not going out again tonight, are you? You know I don't like being in on my own.

7. GREG:     Stop being so stupid, Susan!

8. SUSAN:     (TO HERSELF) I do wish he wouldn't use so many sibilants. It's not very nice to be spattered. I try to wipe it off discreetly - not to hurt his feelings, but . . .

9. GREG:     I don't know why you've got so jumpy lately.

10. SUSAN:     I told you - bad memories.

1. GREG:    Oh, you're not going to start on about your mother!

2. SUSAN:   I can't help it, Greg. Julia coming back has made me think about it all again. Oh, Julia was so good to me when I lost my Mum. She was only fifteen herself, but she knew how to comfort me.

3. GREG:    Yes, she's . . . . (CAJOLING) Look, Susan, you've got to put the past behind you. And I think turning this place into a hotel would help you.

4. SUSAN:   But this is my home, Greg, this house you call 'the mausoleum'! And what do you mean, a hotel - I thought you said a guest house!

5. GREG:    (LOSING PATIENCE) We'll talk about it later.

           <u>(OPENS THE DOOR)</u>

           And don't just sit listening to your mother's old records while I'm out tonight, do something useful like signing those cheques, and that letter to the bank manager!

6. SUSAN:   (SIGHS TO HERSELF) There speaks the master!

           (TO GREG) What time will you be back?

7. GREG:    No idea! Does it matter?

8. SUSAN:   No. I just thought I'd leave some supper out for you, if you're going to be late.

           (TO HERSELF) It's time they added the vow of hypocrisy to the wedding service, don't you think?

1. SUSAN: It wasn't till I married Greg that I understood why my mother used to be pleased when my Dad "found another interest". "If he's bothering them, he's not bothering me," she used to say. She never was explicit. She wasn't miserable, my mother, but she wasn't happy.

PAUSE

My mother didn't believe in divorce. She considered it a humiliation for the woman.

SHE CHANGES THE TAPE TO SINATRA.

She always used to say she was all right as long as she had Sinatra.

MUSIC:   SINATRA 'FLY ME TO THE MOON'

## SCENE 2.

MUSIC:   PAPER ROSES

SUSAN AND JULIA ARE IN THE KITCHEN
HAVING A CUP OF TEA. A TAP DRIPS.
THE WINDOW RATTLES.

1. JULIA:  Mind if I have another choccy biccy? I know I shouldn't, but . . .

2. SUSAN:  Go on. You look wonderful - you always have done.

3. JULIA:  Oh, it's only real friends that tell you lies like that! (TAKES A BISCUIT, BEGINS TO EAT) Ooh, when Greg re-fits this kitchen, it'll be marvellous.

4. SUSAN:  (SIGHS) I suppose so.

5. JULIA:  Susan Danby, what is the matter with you?

6. SUSAN:  Greg's determined to change everything.

7. JULIA:  Well, it needs changing. I couldn't believe it when I saw this place again - the same curtains you had over thirty years ago!

8. SUSAN:  My mother chose them. They were very expensive.

9. JULIA:  You must let Greg go ahead. He's right, you know, it will make a super guest house, and even a hotel if you let Greg extend it!

10. SUSAN:  But it's not my sort of thing, Julia. I'm not sociable like you.

11. JULIA:  (PAUSE) Well - I think it's all wonderful!

1. SUSAN: (TO HERSELF) Julia always was good at enthusiasm. I'm always so hesitant about things. That's one of the problems of being born under the sign of the crab. I got into horoscopes a few months ago. I'd been a bit depressed, so I bought myself a magazine to cheer myself up. There was a four page spread by this astrologer called Dorothea. And it was amazing how accurate she was. So I started reading her horoscopes, to get a bit of insight into my destiny.

2. JULIA: Ah, what's the matter, chicken? It's not just the house, is it?

3. SUSAN: No. It's Greg. I can't seem to please him at all at the moment.

4. JULIA: Oh. I'd have thought he was easy to please. (LAUGHS, COVERING UP) I mean, all men are, aren't they - when it comes, you know, down to it!

5. SUSAN: He's fed up with me, Julia. Sometimes, I think he'd like to get rid of me if it wasn't for my money.

6. JULIA: Now, don't be silly. I'm sure you're imagining all this. You always did have too much imagination.

7. SUSAN: Yes. But now my imagination's fifty years old it has a wider range.

8. JULIA: Now Susan, let's not talk numbers! It scares the life out of me - not to mention the libido!

PAUSE.

1. JULIA: (CALCULATING) Susan, how about if I help you with the house, help you choose new curtains and everything.

2. SUSAN: Oh, would you! Oh, thank you, Julia, I'll enjoy it with you - I've always enjoyed everything with you!

(TO HERSELF) That's true. And yet you could say Julia is the cause of my depression. It's not her fault - she's always been a true friend to me. No, it's the way Greg's been making eyes at her. Oh, there's nothing between them, Julia wouldn't . . . she used to be like a sister to me.But, it's the way he is when she's around. Lively, and well, sexy, I suppose.He's never been like that for me.

3. JULIA: We'll go round the shops tomorrow!

4. SUSAN: Oh, yes! - just like we did when we were teenagers! (PAUSE) I have missed you, you know!

5. JULIA: And I've missed you! I don't know why I didn't keep in touch.

6. SUSAN: I'm so glad you moved back up here after Mike died.

7. JULIA: To be honest, I didn't have much choice.

8. SUSAN: Are you all right, financially?

1. JULIA:     Oh, you know me - always waiting for a
              millionaire to come along and bail me out!

2. SUSAN:     (TO HERSELF) She said her last husband was
              the best one she'd ever had. She seemed a bit
              frightened when she wrote to me. Not very nice,
              losing another husband. And, like she said,
              they're not as easy to replace as you get older.

              (TO JULIA) I'm sure you'll meet someone - you
              always do!

3. JULIA:     Yes. I've been lucky - sometimes. Oh, why do we
              need men, eh?

4. SUSAN:     To look after us. I thought no-one would ever
              marry me. And then Greg made the offer.

              (TO HERSELF) And I accepted it! No fool like a
              frustrated spinster, is there!

              (TO JULIA) You must have been very surprised
              when you found I was married to somebody as
              good looking as Greg.

5. JULIA:     (LYING) No. I was pleased for you.

              PAUSE

6. SUSAN:     To be honest, I've come to realise my money
              played a big part. And I think I panicked really -
              having just lost my father. I was frightened of
              being on my own.

1. JULIA: Yes. I don't like it. I should have come back here to live with you when your Dad died. That was what we used to dream about, wasn't it, when we were kids?

2. SUSAN: Yes. But you'd got married.

3. JULIA: Yes. Again! (LAUGHS) Never learn, do I?

4. SUSAN: Don't you ever get tired of being - with men?

5. JULIA: (BRIGHTENING) Ooh, no!

6. SUSAN: (TO HERSELF) That's always been a big difference between me and Julia. She's always been a one for the men. And they all love her - well, she's got so much to offer. I must look up her star sign - her birthday's in May, so she's Taurus, or Gemini. Must be Taurus,

"they frequently make disastrous mistakes in their love life, and are ardent and fascinating lovers." Yes, definitely Taurus.

I've never been ardent, I don't think. I used to have my dreams - like any other young girl, but . . . . I was never pretty enough to be passionate. And Greg has never been . . .

7. JULIA: Shall we have a look round, and talk about what needs doing?

8. SUSAN: Yes, all right.

## SCENE 3.

MUSIC:   TRUE LOVE (HIGH SOCIETY)

THE HALL AND STAIRCASE (CARPET ON
THE STAIRS). A GRANDFATHER CLOCK
TICKS LOUDLY THEN CHIMES THREE.

1. JULIA:     (STARTLED) Oh, that flaming clock! Honestly,
Susan - this house, it's like a posh funeral
parlour!

2. SUSAN:     You didn't use to think so! You used to envy me,
living here!

3. JULIA:     I still do! I wish I'd had parents with a big house
and money to leave to me!

4. SUSAN:     (TO HERSELF) Julia's never had it easy.

(TO JULIA) Mind you don't catch those heels in
this old carpet. I still don't know how you
manage to walk in those shoes and that tight
skirt.

5. JULIA:     Oh, give over! The day I stop wearing sexy
clothes they can put me in my box!

6. SUSAN:     I never did have the courage to wear anything
eye-catching, did I?

7. JULIA:     No. Remember the struggle I had to get you into
a mini skirt! And nobody laughed, did they?

8. SUSAN:     My Dad did, before he got nasty about it.

1. JULIA:     Oh, well - your Dad!

<u>THEY WALK ALONG THE LANDING.</u>

2. SUSAN:     I think you were right, you know, I should have left home. I should have done a lot of things. I'm only just learning that now.

3. JULIA:     You should have learned years ago - I was willing to teach you!

4. SUSAN:     I know. You've always been so good to me, Julia. From the moment you arrived at our school, and rescued me from the bullies, you've been special.

5. JULIA:     (WISTFUL) That was all a long time ago, love.

(OPENING A DOOR) Ooh, is this the master bedroom?

## SCENE 4.

THE KITCHEN. SOUNDS OF WASHING
UP. GREG BANGS HIS FIST ON THE
DRAINING BOARD, MAKING CROCKERY
JUMP.

1. GREG:    Why can't you understand? It'll be a good
investment!

2. SUSAN:   It's a lot of money. And I've told you, I'm not
sure about it.

3. GREG:    When were you ever sure about anything!
(PAUSE)

I'm an easy man to please, Susan. Why can't
you make me happy, give me what I want?

4. SUSAN:   I thought I did when I married you.

(TO HERSELF) But Greg is Aries, you see - the
ram.

(PAUSE. SUSAN CLEARS HER THROAT)

5. GREG:    (PERSUASIVE) Look, Susan, I've told you, it's
only short term. When things really start
moving again, I'll sell those houses I built at
Stanton and pay you back. Come on, love.

6. SUSAN:   (TO HERSELF) Oh, it's different when he wants
something - then it's all "come close and breathe
me in!" I'm not falling for that again!

(TO GREG) I've told you, I'm not keen on the
idea of turning my home into a hotel.

7. GREG:    You're never 'keen'!

1. SUSAN:    (TO HERSELF) Greg's horoscope said he would resent opposition to his plans this week. One of the characteristics of Aries is that they are ambitious, and that they like a good time. Greg chose Torremolinos for "a good time" this year. Topless bathing. You know.

2. GREG:    Think about it. I know what I'm doing. I always have done, haven't I?

3. SUSAN:    (SARCASTIC) Oh, yes!

4. GREG:    Oh, I'm going!

EXIT - SLAMS THE DOOR.

5. SUSAN:    (TO HERSELF) Aries again. Tend to react aggressively to any opposition. I've learned a lot about him, studying his horoscope.

SHE OPENS A MAGAZINE.

It's been a comfort to me in a way - I used to think everything was my fault.

## SCENE 5.

MUSIC:   NAT KING COLE "A BLOSSOM
FELL"

THE LOUNGE. SUSAN PICKS UP THE
TELEPHONE. SHE DIALS A NUMBER.
JULIA ANSWERS.

1. JULIA:      Hello? Is that you?

2. SUSAN:      Yes, it's Susan. I was wondering if you'd like to
come round.

3. JULIA:      Oh, of course, I'd love to, pet! When were you
thinking of?

4. SUSAN:      Well, now, actually. This evening. Greg's out.
We've had a row - just like Dorothea predicted.
Opposition and deceit she said I'd have to face
this week.

5. JULIA:      Oh. You're not still reading that nonsense are
you? What was this row about?

6. SUSAN:      Money for his hotel idea.

7. JULIA:      Oh. Well, you'd get it back when he sells those
houses.

8. SUSAN:      Has he told you about those?

9. JULIA:      Oh. He just mentioned it - when he came round
to see about my central heating.

(HASTILY) It was ever so kind of him to come all
the way over here and fix it. I think he feels
sorry for me - being on my own.

10. SUSAN:  Yes. (PAUSE) He can be . . sympathetic

PAUSE

1. JULIA:    Are you all right?

2. SUSAN:    No. He's making me miserable, Julia, just like my Dad used to. If I wasn't so scared of being on my own again, I'd leave him.

3. JULIA:    Would you? (PAUSE) Well, perhaps you ought to think about it. I'm sure you'd be all right in a nice little flat.

4. SUSAN:    No, I wouldn't like that. He wouldn't divorce me anyway - he needs my money at the moment.

5. JULIA:    Yes.

6. SUSAN:    Anyway, he's gone out again, and I could do with some company. Can you come round?

7. JULIA:    No. I'm sorry, love, but I can't. Not this evening.

8. SUSAN:    Oh. Are you sure? We could work on the kitchen design Greg wanted.

F/X JULIA'S DOOR BELL RINGS.

9. JULIA:    Yes. Look, I'm expecting, a visitor.

10. SUSAN:    (TEASING) Ooh! Anyone I know?

THE DOOR BELL RINGS AGAIN.

11. JULIA:    No! No, of course not! Susan, I've got to go.He's here. See you soon!

SHE RINGS OFF.

1. SUSAN:     (TO HERSELF) Lucky Julia!

               SHE PUTS THE PHONE DOWN.

2. SUSAN:     (SIGHS) So, another evening on my own, trying not to hear strange noises. I'm not going to take a tablet though.

               (GETS UP AND WALKS ACROSS TO THE DRINKS CABINET)

I'll have a whisky instead!

               SHE POURS HERSELF A DRINK.

I find I don't need the tablets as often since I started to consult Dorothea. And since I've got my Julia back again. She's the only person who's ever made me feel really happy. I was fairly happy with Greg at first, but I've come to realise - he's a bully really, and, I don't think he cares about me any more - if he ever did.

Julia says men like you to show your gratitude. But I'm not very good at showing anything - not that I've much to show. Some women spread nicely in their middle years, get more cuddly - like Julia. And some women do the opposite. Like me. I looked at myself in the bedroom mirror the other evening when I was getting changed. Grey flesh sagging in the sunset.

I put the light on, but it didn't help! I mustn't let things get me down, though. In my next week's horoscope Dorothea's promised romantic intrigue - sounds exciting, doesn't it? Perhaps I'll meet someone at the bridge club.

## SCENE 6.

THE LOUNGE. SINATRA SINGS "IT'S ALL
RIGHT WITH ME". JULIA SINGS ALONG
WITH THE TAPE.

1. JULIA:     I can't believe you've still got your mother's old radiogram! I always liked her records though. Sinatra, Nat King Cole. So romantic!

2. GREG:     Let me fill your glass up, Julia.

        POURS MORE WINE INTO HER GLASS

3. JULIA:     Oh, isn't he naughty, Susan!

4. SUSAN:     He likes to think he's a good host. (TO HERSELF) And he likes to have the excuse to lean over her. Look at him, touching her! He's almost got his tongue hanging out!

5. JULIA:     (GIGGLES) Ooh, Greg! Stop it!

6. SUSAN:     (TO HERSELF) And she's playing up to it. She can't help herself - she's always reacted to men. (TO GREG) Could I have some more wine, too, Greg?

7. GREG:     Oh. Sorry. Mustn't neglect the wife, eh, Julia?

8. JULIA:     No.

        SHE BEGINS TO SING AGAIN, AND THEN
        GETS UP AND STARTS TO DANCE
        ROUND.

Come on! Let's have a dance! Can't waste these floor boards! You'll have the new carpet down next time I come. Can't dance on carpet!

1. SUSAN:    Oh, yes, come on, Greg - we haven't danced together since we were courting.

2. GREG:    No. Get off!

3. SUSAN:    (ANNOYED) Well, if you won't dance with me, dance with Julia. It's only manners to entertain your guests!

4. JULIA:    Now, now, you two!

5. SUSAN:    Go on, Greg. Enjoy yourself!

6. JULIA:    (FEELING AWKWARD) We can all have a good time!

7. SUSAN:    Can we? I'm just going to the bathroom.

8. GREG:    (HEAVING HIMSELF UP) Oh, well, come on then, Julia, a quick twirl then. Anything to keep the ladies happy!

9. JULIA:    Oh, Greg!

10. SUSAN:    (CLOSING THE DOOR) I'll bring the supper things when I come back.

(TO HERSELF) Look at him! Look at the way he's running his hands over her body. He's never done that to me.

SHE CLOSES THE DOOR AND PAUSES BEFORE SHE GOES UP THE STAIRS, HEARING JULIA AND GREG LAUGHING.

11. JULIA:    Takes a lot more than a quick twirl to keep me happy!

SHE AND GREG LAUGH TOGETHER.

## SCENE 7.

THE LANDING. TOILET FLUSHED IN THE
BATHROOM. IN THE LOUNGE SINATRA IS
SINGING "YOU'RE SENSATIONAL" SUSAN
COMES OUT OF THE BATHROOM,
CLOSES THE DOOR AND STARTS TO
WALK BACK DOWNSTAIRS. THE MUSIC
ENDS. SUSAN PAUSES AS SHE HEARS
GREG AND JULIA FROM THE LOUNGE.

1. JULIA:    Ooh, Greg!

2. GREG:    Go on!

3. JULIA:    (LAUGHING) No! Get off! She'll be back in a minute!

JULIA SQUEALS AND GIGGLES.

4. SUSAN:    (TO HERSELF) I wish I'd walked straight past the door on my way to the kitchen. I wish I hadn't seen them! Oh, Julia!

## SCENE 8.

### THE LOUNGE. NO MORE MUSIC.

1. SUSAN: Help yourself. I'll get the vol au vents - they're in the oven.

2. JULIA: Ooh, lovely! Shall I put another record on?

3. SUSAN: Haven't you danced enough for one night?

4. JULIA: Oh . . .

### SUSAN EXITS, BANGING THE DOOR A LITTLE. FADE UP.

5. JULIA: No, Greg. you won't want me here on your birthday. You'll want a candlelit dinner for two, won't you?

6. SUSAN: (TO HERSELF) Candlelit dinners - she knows all about those. She's had all the love and romance I've never had. And now she's got Greg!

(TO JULIA) Oh, no. I think Greg will want you for his birthday, won't you, Greg dear?

7. GREG: Well . . .

8. SUSAN: We'll have a special meal and forget all about the doctor's diet. I've decided all this low cholesterol business is a waste of time!

9. JULIA: Oh, I think Greg should be careful.

10. SUSAN: It's the week after next, his birthday.The second of April.

11. JULIA: Yes.

12. SUSAN: When's your birthday, Julia?

## SCENE 9.

KITCHEN. GREG AND SUSAN ARE
HAVING BREAKFAST. GREG EATS
ENTHUSIASTICALLY.

1. SUSAN: (TO HERSELF) A cooked breakfast every morning now. No porridge, though, far too good for him!

   (TO GREG) Another slice of fried bread, Greg?

2. GREG: Yes, all right. (SERVED) Ta. Susan, I went to the bank again, yesterday.

3. SUSAN: Oh, yes?

4. GREG: I need that money from you soon. It's holding things up.

5. SUSAN: There's no rush. By the way, the new lounge curtains have arrived at last. Julia's coming round tomorrow to put them up for me.

6. GREG: (OVER INNOCENT) Oh, is she?

7. SUSAN: (TO HERSELF) As if you didn't know her every movement - you and your dancing partner!

   Julia's birthday's May 31st. Gemini. You can't depend on Geminis. When I look back through my personal horoscope,I can see that Dorothea was trying to warn me.

8. GREG: You can cash in some of your Dad's shares. You won't miss them.

9. SUSAN: Oh?

1. SUSAN:  (TO HERSELF) Greg doesn't give up. When he wants something he goes all out to get it. Aries again. They impose their will on others. Some women like it, apparently.

(TO GREG) No, Greg. I'm not selling any shares.

2. GREG:  For god's sake, why not?

3. SUSAN:  Because they're mine, not yours, and I'll do what I want with them - not what you want!

(TO HERSELF) Doesn't sound like a timid, hesitant crab, does it? But Dorothea's revealed that there's more to my personality than I thought.

4. GREG:  I'm wasting my time talking to you these days!.

(STRIDES TO THE DOOR AND OPENS IT)

A wife is supposed to support her husband, help him! You do nothing for me - in any department.

PAUSE

5. SUSAN:  (ANGRY) Oh, really? (PAUSE) Going out, are we?

6. GREG:  We are! I've just about had as much as I can take of you!

7. SUSAN:  The golf club again?

8. GREG:  Yes!

9. SUSAN:  (TO HERSELF) It's on the way to Julia's. He used to have a drink there first - to back up his story but he doesn't even bother about an alibi now. I don't like that - him being so flagrant about it.

1. SUSAN: (TO HERSELF) I couldn't bear people to laugh at me. At school, they used to laugh at me - before Julia stopped them.

> GREG BANGS THE FRONT DOOR. CAR
>
> TYRES SCREECH AS HE DRIVES OFF AT
>
> SPEED.

2. SUSAN: (TO HERSELF) I wouldn't have let Greg have a fast car like that at one time - not the way he drives. I bought it for him for his birthday. I prefer something you can wrap, really. But it was what he wanted.

   Men seem to always know what they want, don't they? And they get it, while we're still making our minds up. I'm beginning to think that's the secret of male dominance.

   I've started thinking quite a bit, since Dorothea put me on the right track. She says that, in this my fiftieth year, I should take a firm hold on my destiny and find the excitement and happiness I have always longed for.

## SCENE 10.

THE LOUNGE. MUSIC:    "JEZEBEL"
FRANKIE LANE

JULIA IS STANDING ON STEPS, HANGING
CURTAINS. SHE SLIDES HOOKS ALONG
THE RAIL.

1. JULIA:     I'm not keen on Frankie Lane.

2. SUSAN:    Oh. I'll turn it off then. Have you got enough
             hooks?

3. JULIA:     Yes. Is that hanging even?

4. SUSAN:    Yes. Oh, they are beautiful curtains. You were
             absolutely right about the colours.

5. JULIA:     Yes, I like them.

             (PAUSE)

6. SUSAN:    (TO HERSELF) I understand now why Julia was
             so keen to help me choose everything.

7. JULIA:     (DRAWS THE CURTAINS ALONG) How's that
             look?

8. SUSAN:    Wonderful! Now come down and I'll get you a
             drink. Gin and tonic?

             (TO HERSELF) I don't want to blame Julia. She
             always has been - vulnerable, that way. So I
             haven't said anything to her. And actually,
             Cancerians can gain a lot from the company of
             Geminis, if they know how to handle them. No,
             I've no intention of losing Julia.

## FADE UP. ICE CHINKS IN GLASSES.

1. JULIA: So, do you agree - pink and ivory in the master bedroom.

2. SUSAN: Yes, that sounds all right. It's funny, isn't it, that it's still referred to as the master's bedroom. We can't have come as far as we thought, can we?

3. JULIA: Oh, you're not going to start on about women's lib, are you? That was played out in the eighties.

4. SUSAN: Oh, I missed it, then. (PAUSE) Well, perhaps I can have a go on my own.

## SCENE 11.

### THE LOUNGE.

1. SUSAN:    What do you think of the curtains, Greg?

2. GREG;    Marvellous! She's got style, has your friend, Julia.

3. SUSAN:    Yes. I'm glad you appreciate her.

4. GREG:    Oh, I do!

5. JULIA:    (COY) Well, I'm pleased you like them, Greg.

6. GREG:    Thank you, sweetheart.

           ### (KISSES JULIA WITH PASSION).

7. JULIA:    (EMBARRASSED) Greg!

8. SUSAN:    (TO HERSELF) Yes, quite flagrant. Well, you see, he's sold a couple of those houses, so he's got some money again.

           (TO GREG & JULIA) I'll see how that casserole is doing.

           ### SHE EXITS, AND HALF CLOSES THE DOOR. BUT BEFORE SHE WALKS AWAY, SHE HEARS GREG AND JULIA EMBRACE.

9. JULIA:    Ooh, Greg!

10. SUSAN:   (TO HERSELF - LISTENING BY THE DOOR) They hardly wait till I'm out of the room these days.

1. GREG: You will come this weekend? She knows it's the Builders' Conference, so there's no problem. A whole weekend, Julia!

2. JULIA: I don't know if I should.

3. GREG: Oh, please! I'll talk to the solicitor when we come back, I promise!

4. JULIA: Oh. All right, then.

5. SUSAN: (TO HERSELF) So, he's decided what he wants, has he? Oh, Greg.

6. JULIA: Oh, I feel awful about Susan. But I do want you, Greg!

THEY KISS PASSIONATELY.

7. SUSAN: (UPSET) He's never kissed me like that! Never held me with that sort of passion! He's cheated me! He took my money and gave me nothing!

## SCENE 12.

ON THE DRIVE GREG REVS UP THE CAR
ENGINE.

1. JULIA:     (FORCED BRIGHTNESS) Goodnight, Susan! I'll
make sure he comes straight back after he's
taken me home!

2. SUSAN:     (WITH IRONY) Thank you.

3. JULIA:     (EMBARRASSED) You watch that video I
brought. It's a lovely musical High Society.

4. SUSAN:     I might have an early night.

5. JULIA:     Yes. You do look a bit tired.Well, good night,
love!

SHE SLAMS THE CAR DOOR.

THEY DRIVE AWAY.

6. SUSAN:     (TO HERSELF) She does care about me in her
way. And now Greg's going to take her away
from me. (PAUSE) If I let him.

(PAUSE)

It's a characteristic of those born under the sign
of the crab - when they make their minds up
that they really want something - they're very
tenacious and stop at nothing to achieve their
aim!

## SCENE 13.

THE LOUNGE. HARRY SECOMBE

RECORD, TRACK

'KATHARINE'(IS THERE NO MERCY IN

YOUR UNFORGIVING HEART)

SUSAN POURS HERSELF A DRINK.

1. SUSAN:     I don't usually drink before lunchtime.Not like
              Greg. he thinks he's running late if he hasn't
              had one by eleven. I've stopped telling Greg his
              horoscope. He wasn't interested anyway. Men
              are too ready to laugh at that sort of thing. Greg
              says horoscopes are only right if you make them
              come true.

              (SHE GIVES A LITTLE LAUGH)

              I must get some more whisky. I don't like Greg
              to be without his whisky.

## SCENE 14.

THE LOUNGE. WHISKY POURED INTO A

GLASS.

1. GREG:    (SLIGHTLY DRUNK) No, Susan. Not after I've
downed nearly a full bottle of wine!

2. SUSAN:    But Greg, it's that whisky you've been looking
for, the special malt you had in Scotland.

3. GREG:    Really? Yes, that's the one! Go on, then, "just a
wee dram!"

SUSAN LAUGHS AS SHE POURS A LARGE

DRINK GREG DRINKS NOISILY

4. GREG:    Oh, superb! (SUSAN POURS MORE INTO HIS
GLASS) No! Well, just one more, then. I've got to
go in a minute, though.

5. SUSAN:    Oh, yes. Mustn't miss your night at "the golf
club". It's the first time you've had the chance
all week, isn't it? What with one thing and
another.

6. GREG:    Yes.

SUSAN POURS AGAIN, AND ONE FOR

HERSELF.

7. GREG:    (SURPRISED) Are you having one?

8. SUSAN:    Yes. Even I need a drink sometimes!(PAUSE)
Come on, one for the road!

CAR SPEEDING

MUSIC: "UNFORGETTABLE"

# SCENE 15.

## INSIDE A CHURCH. 23RD PSALM IS BEING SUNG.

## JULIA WEEPS NOISILY.

1. SUSAN: I suppose I could blame myself for Greg's death if I wanted to. After all I bought him the car, and the whisky. And the roads are always busy on Friday night. People rushing off to "have a good time".

But it's all down to your stars in the end, really - isn't it?. Greg should have read his horoscope, like I did, then perhaps he wouldn't have gone.

Under Aries it said, "Avoid all unnecessary journeys".Of course, he hadn't seen Julia all week - and when the flesh drives, well, a tree on a dark country lane doesn't stand a chance, does it?

## EXTRA LOUD SOB FROM JULIA

She's very upset. It's quite embarrassing.I've sold the rest of those houses Greg built - for quite a good price, actually.

## JULIA'S SOBBING INTERRUPTS AGAIN

(SIGHS, A BIT EXASPERATED) I think she'll get over it fairly quickly when she's heard my offer. Gemini's are like that - capable of dispassionate judgement. She's always done what was to her advantage, has Julia.

## SCENE 16.

THE LOUNGE. IN THE DISTANCE
TAPPING AND HAMMERING. CLOSE TO
THE MIC SUSAN IS UNPACKING PLATES
AND CUPS. A LIGHT KNOCK AT THE
DOOR.

1. JULIA:     Can I come in?

2. SUSAN:     Yes. The dinner plates and coffee cups have
              arrived. I'm just checking it all.

3. JULIA:     I've made us a nice fresh salmon salad for
              lunch. Is that all right?

4. SUSAN:     Lovely. I do hope they're going to finish laying
              the carpet in the bar soon.

5. JULIA:     Oh, is the banging giving you a headache? I'll
              have a word with them.

              SHE EXITS.

6. SUSAN:     (TO HERSELF) She does look after me, does
              Julia. She always did - when it suited her.

              PAUSE.

              The Fortuna hotel we've called it. Greg's money
              has come in very handy, paying for the
              alterations and furnishings. It's going to be very
              elegant and luxurious. My mother would have
              been pleased. She always got a lot of
              satisfaction out of spending my Dad's money on
              the house.

1. SUSAN:     (TO HERSELF) Julia is thrilled to be manageress, especially on the sort of salary I'm paying.

              (SHE STACKS THE LAST OF THE

              PLATES.)

              I think she's quite relieved really that she'll never have to look for a husband again.

              JULIA ENTERS AGAIN.

2. JULIA:     I forgot to tell you. I've made us appointments at the hairdresser's for Wednesday afternoon. If that's convenient?

3. SUSAN:     Yes, fine. And we'll go shopping afterwards. I've seen a rather chic little dress in Annabel's.

              (TO HERSELF) I'm having a perm. Julia thinks it will make me look a lot younger. I'm paying for her to have a re-style too. It'll cheer her up. She still gets a bit down when she thinks of Greg.

4. JULIA:     (HESITANT) Susan, shall we call in at a travel agents on the way to the hairdresser's? Like you said, it would be nice to have a little holiday before we open. Spain's very cheap at the moment. We could have a smashing week in somewhere like Torremolinos.

5. SUSAN:     No. Not Torremolinos. I've always wanted to go to Florence, or Vienna.

6. JULIA:     (NOT ENTHUSIASTIC) Oh.

1. SUSAN:    And Julia. There's something I've been meaning
             to mention. Will you not call me Susan any
             more? Make it Sue. Much lighter and brighter,
             don't you think? More suitable for a hostess?

2. JULIA:    Yes.

3. SUSAN:    (TO HERSELF) I found a book on names and the
             influence they have over your character. For
             Julia, it says 'dazzling, amorous and
             superficial'. I think they got that about right.

             Susans need someone to advise and help them.
             That's why I've got Julia here. She's going to run
             the hotel, while I play the hostess - I'll chat to
             interesting guests, that sort of thing. And I've
             never wanted to be on my own.There you are,
             timid Cancerian again!Like Dorothea predicted,
             this was the year I had to make a new life for
             myself, before it was too late.

             <u>SHE SELECTS A TAPE AND PUTS IT ON</u>

             <u>THE RADIOGRAM</u>

             She was so right! I've sent her a cheque, as a
             thank you. And as a kind of final payment.

             <u>A STRAUSS WALTZ BEGINS.</u>

4. SUSAN:    Dorothea's given me the sort of guidance I
             needed over the past few months, but I think
             that, in a way, you have to learn to make your
             own destiny in the end, don't you?

             <u>FADE UP THE WALTZ. SUSAN LA LAS</u>

             <u>JOYOUSLY.</u>

## *Other Scripts by Liz Wainwright*

| | |
|---|---|
| Does Your Mother Dance? | Stage Play – black comedy |
| Mixed Company | Stage Play – black comedy |
| Grounded | Stage Monologue |
| One in Three | TV Film |
| Sunshine | Radio Drama |
| Gwyn | Radio Drama |

www.lizscript.co.uk